T4-AKN-874

THE DAY DALI DIED

Other Books by the Author

The Book of Frog
Lyric of the Highway Mariner (poetry)
Dradin, In Love
The Book of Lost Places
The Early History of Ambergris
The Exchange
City of Saints & Madmen
Veniss Underground

THE DAY DALI DIED

POETRY AND FLASH FICTION

JEFF VANDERMEER

PRIME BOOKS
Canton, Ohio

THE DAY DALI DIED

Copyright © 2003 by **Jeff VanderMeer**
Cover art copyright © 2003 by **Hawk Alfredson**
Cover design copyright © 2003 by **Garry Nurrish**
Thanks to **Mark Roberts** for technical assistance.

These poems and stories first appeared in *Amazing Stories, AS Magazine, The Book of Frog, Dark Voices 5, Deathrealm, Departures, Electric Velocipede, Ellipsis, Libraries of Thought and the Imagination, The Mangrove Review, Nebula Awards 30, The New York Review of SF, Piddiddle Poetry Magazine, The Plaza, Pulphouse, The Silver Web, Starshore, The Third Alternative,* and the poetry collection *Lyric of the Highway Mariner.* "Seagull," "Fiji," and "The Ship at the End of the World," are previously unpublished.

All rights reserved. No part of this publication may be reproduced or transmitted in any form or by any means, electronic or mechanical, including photocopy, recording, or any information storage and retrieval system now known or invented, without permission in writing from the publisher, except by a reviewer who wishes to quote brief passages in connection with a review written for inclusion in a magazine, newspaper, broadcast, etc.

Published in the United States by **Prime Books, Inc.**
P.O. Box 36503, Canton, OH 44735
www.primebooks.net

Trade Paperback **ISBN** 1-894815-92-0
Hardcover **ISBN** 1-894815-93-9

For my siblings:

Elizabeth, François, and Nicholas

CONTENTS

9   INTRODUCTION

POETRY
13   The Ministry of Whimsy
15   Lassie
16   We Underground
17   Bastille Sangfroid
19   The Day Dali Died
20   Gilligan's Island Revisited
22   The Disappearance of Dogcatchers
24   Death by Drowning
25   Flight Is For Those Who Have Not Yet Crossed Over
27   Baobab
31   Seagull
32   Fiji
34   The Pigs of Guinea
36   Trees and Houses
38   Sentinels
39   Four Theories of Earth-Moon System Formation
43   An Afterlife
54   The Ship At the Edge of the World

FICTION

59 The Songs a Dead Whale Sings

63 The Flower Vendor

66 The Country Fair

71 Kaeru

79 A Social Gathering

84 A Few Notes Upon Finding a Green Alien Baby Figure . . .

90 Bullets and Airplanes

101 Henry Dreams of Angkor Wat

105 A Brief Summary of Seven Lost Books

111 At the Crossroads, Burying the Dog

INTRODUCTION

I write my way into short stories and novels through the texture of the language. When I've achieve the correct density or layering effect in the opening sentences, I know I can write the rest of the story. With poetry and short-short fiction, this process is intensified and condensed—plot and character rendered down into their essential images and moments. As a result, readers get different pleasures from poetry and short-short fiction. They cannot expect the same types of complexities and character interactions. They can, however, expect the sudden illumination of a moment or a scene. They can expect a surreal character study. They can expect the evocation of a county fair (for example).

Although I rarely write poetry these days, I continue to write poetic prose—prose that often pays attention to meter, to slant rhyme, and similar poetic techniques. These short-short, or flash, fictions provide me with the closest sensation to a poetic release. They also allow me to experiment with non-traditional structures, which can be liberating.

Many of these poems and stories have an interesting history as well. The poem "Flight Is For Those . . . " not only won a

Rhysling Award—it became a full-blown short story. The poem "The Ministry of Whimsy" gave me the eventual title of the publishing company I have run for the past fifteen years. "Four Theories of Earth-Moon System Formation" was my first professional sale, to *Amazing Stories*. I wrote it while attending an Astronomy class at the University of Florida. I dropped the class, but I got a poem out of it. "An Afterlife" was one of the earliest poems I ever wrote—an ambitious, perhaps overly-serious epic whose individual sections have appeared in various poetry journals over the years. Although "Fiji" appears here for the first time, I have previously stolen lines from it, transformed, for various personal essays.

As for the fiction, "The Songs a Dead Whale Sings" is a riff on (some might say pastiche of) Ballard's short story about a drowned giant. "Henry Dreams of Angkor Wat" is one of the first stories my now-wife Ann published in her *Silver Web* magazine, and still one of my personal favorites. "Kaeru," pulled from my first collection, *The Book of Frog*, mixes haiku and Japanese mythology. "A Few Notes . . ." is a nod to the alien baby photographs on my Web site (see below).

But let me be as brief as the work you are about to read: I hope you like this collection of moments, lines, and charged images. Thank you for reading.

- *Jeff VanderMeer*, **May 2003**
vanderworld@hotmail.com
http://www.vanderworld.redsine.com

POETRY

THE MINISTRY OF WHIMSY

Patient with other patients
but a horror to the staff
Tony times his outbursts
to the minute, launches tirades
with bubbly indignation.
Mindwise, he's a waste;
he's always thought
he was a Scottish prince
who might have ascended the throne
but for the intervention of Parliament.
"Bring me kilts!
Bring me bagpipes!
Bring me boots
to clothe my feet
and a brogue to curse them with!"

Sean just saw
One Flew Over the Cuckoo's Nest.
Now he's not so sure he's insane.
He rests his head against a pillow,
reciting a sane man's lines:
hooks to catch the warden on.
He thinks he's a devil-may-care,
affects the airs of a "Here's Johnny!"
or hardnosed mafia man.
(Nicholson's his Santa come
Christmas time.)

Pretty waif Peggy pretends
she's not really here,

blind as she is
and hard of hearing.
The pigs of guinea,
myths of shadowed memory,
jaunt through her mind,
through her mouth.
She has told her stories
three times over to every
single ministry member;
their heads ring
with palmistry and piggery,
eclipses and the dead eyes
of sailors staring
from the earth.
They croon and caterwaul
while Peggy smiles
all unknowing.

Light glints off the windows,
the red brick walls,
the faces inside pale moons
too soon new.

LASSIE
(the lost episode)

Lassie, gone insane
under the bright lights
of retake after retake
hates litul kids
loathes the milk-soft smell,
the screaming/singing/crying,
the tug-tug on fur,
repetitious games of tag
under the apple tree.
She's tired of rescuing
Petey and Shirley
from

> owls
> horses
> flash floods
> major earthquakes
> international terrorists

Lassie revels in the taste
of flesh, the cool white feel,
the peeling back of skin
(such a convenient wrapper).
If only, if only—she wags her tail,
looks up into their faces—
they can be fattened up,
then there will be no need for ratings,
only teeth and guile.

WE UNDERGROUND

among the sweating moles,
among the digging worms
hear the river chuckling bright.

the owl cannot see us,
though we feel its shadow
across the moonglow grasses;
we listen to the tread of feet,
smell light, just out of reach.

when we speak
it is the wind trickling
through grass,
through earth.

when forgotten,
the rivers become our arteries,
carrying dislodged memories,
collarbones floating
to the surface like
questionmarks.

BASTILLE SANGFROID

Fingers of smoke
stroke grass
clutch the hills ahead
carry the stench
of burning flesh.

I wonder
who or what crackles
and hisses far from view
whether a witch wishes
too late to mend her ways
or if it is something
more innocent
a baby perhaps
whose bluing bones
blaze amid the flames
of a cruel baptism.

Laughter
shrill and brittle
brings me to the brink
of abattoir; how far
from blue bones to
Blue Beard?
Perhaps I read
too much into what is
not there.

Winter now
too late for leaves

to release their fear
of falling, too late
for the bonfire's roar.
Yet something screams.

My shoes scuff
the grass in haste.
I will know what lies
beyond the hill
before the sun
rises slothlike
from the bosom
of the dead
the dying.

THE DAY DALI DIED

watches sagged suddenly
on the wrists
of young women

dalmations lost decades
ago reappeared, no longer
mere spots

and critics found
the embryos of tiny
businessmen curled up
in their soft-boiled eggs.

GILLIGAN'S ISLAND REVISITED

The Skipper, weary
of silly Gilligan questions,
silly Gilligan insults,
tears off his friend's right leg,
then the left, with a hearty laugh.
Eager to play boy scout,
the Professor cauterizes
his wounds while the Skipper
cooks the legs over an open fire,
other characters creeping
from the backdrop to gnaw
on Gilligan flesh.

(Later, when the bones have dried,
the Professor will shine them yellow,
caress them, grandiose scenes
of resurrection surfacing in dreams.)

Gilligan, meanwhile,
pulls himself across the sand,
to the beach, weeping over sunsets,
scratching at his ragged stumps.
Every hour the Skipper comes by,
spits on him, says, "Ya look great."

That night, everyone gathers
around a washed-up TV set,
the twilight gloom comfortable,

the gray cracked screen
reflecting the campfire,
the struggles of Gilligan
sans legs.

"Ya know," says the Skipper, "I think
he's funnier this way . . . "

Almost drowning the shrieks,
they lay down laugh track
for the hohaho spectacle
of Gilligan gouging out his eyes,
throwing his sight to the sharks.

(Later, the Professor will fish them
from the ocean, whittle the leg bones
into a parody of human form,
attach the eyes,
and ask this new deity
questions like

What is the half-life of a rerun?)

THE DISAPPEARANCE OF DOGCATCHERS

Eyes corroded circles
ribs countable
skin stretched canvas-taut
they slink from hiding
to join the pack.

When they see us
they do not flinch away,
even those who starve
one or two legs short.

They pad across
tile battlefields where
the gardener has failed.
They sit outside our doors
and greet us with the wagging
of misshapen tails.

We, living in a world
where the only shadows
are the rings round our eyes,
where we soothe ourselves to sleep
by the purr of the refrigerator
the hum of the television screen,
ignore them.

Here,
where the only dogs

are domesticated,
fat and whole.

Where the light
cannot fall
so brightly.

DEATH BY DROWNING

I stand on the gravel beach
where seagulls circle
and scream in hunger
or warning, and I think
about the things you did
to make me the person
I have become in your
absence.

Not a wave mars
the smooth glass surface
of the ocean, as if
oceans age differently
than you and me, as if when
they age, they lose all
their wrinkles and their
gracelessness and drift
into deep slumber, unbroken
by thoughts like these:
that I loved you,
that you are dead,
that you are not
coming back.

Julie, I never
thought I would see
the ocean bleeding
from your eyes.

FLIGHT IS FOR THOSE WHO HAVE NOT YET CROSSED OVER

You never thought
it could happen this way,
in a Guatemalan prison
among men armed
with rubber hoses, scalpels,
piano wire, and propaganda;
men who scream at you
to tell what you cannot tell,
until you mark the days by
the visits of your interrogators,
muttered prayers to God,
and the screams that echo
down the hall.

In a dream on a moonless night
it came to you from beyond the window,
mixed with the smell of palm trees,
sea salt, and rotting wood:
it came to you like a whisper
from your dead lover,
an exhalation of her breath.
You woke sprawled against
the wall opposite your bed
and the guard said, "Dios mio!"
It was a miracle, a visitation,
the work of saints or devils.

You had flown around the cell
like an eagle, your arms
outstretched, fingers reaching
for the sky.

Miraculous, and yet you
laughed along with the guard,
because to fly in your cell
cannot save you, because
the only flight you desire
is the flight of an angel,
spiraling upward, freed
from the sharp, clarifying
edge of pain.

BAOBAB

I.

Up-
rooted,
over-
turned,
the tree
wears a crown
of roots, sucks
sustenance from the sky.

But wood
sighs, sags,
the sky
too heavy
for this Atlas,
the sandy land
too parched;
branches cannot
brace themselves
against both
forever.

II.

Twisted,
twisted
trunk—
a girth that
wears down

even elephant tusks;
wooden nerve ends fray
but pull taut.

Dark scars form
the faces of men;
rotting beards flow
into the grain—
eyes glitter through
the smooth lines.

They watch,
wait, features
eroding,
forgetting,
reforming;
a river of wood
that never runs dry.

III.

Seasons end
and begin.
The tree explodes
in a riot
of inverted form:
blossoms coat branches.

Birds scream
foreign words,
fluster from twig
to twig.
Lions lounge

with insolence.
Insects walk along
grooved bark pathways,
sound too soft to hear,
but building,
building.

At night,
the moon sharpens
to a bloodless scimitar
and bush babies rustle
along secret paths
to pollen.

IV.

And the season
shifts to summer,
a summer of seething heat.

And the sun slavers
with thirst at dawn,
fever unquenched at dusk.

And animals sleep
the dead sleep of drought,
eyes dry and fly-plagued.

And the baobab
is stripped of flowers,
leaves, even bark.

And bush babies ask
the riddle, "What lies
buried under the earth?"

V.

Resurrected
in the sunset of the season,
the baobab supplicates the sky,
light bleeding between branches.
The sky darkens and the wind
speaks in bone-thin voices.

The tree twists
and twists and
twists under rain clouds;
the faces of men in bark
contort, grimace, shift,
sweating with sap.

Drops fall fast
and faster, wrung
from a rag.

Everywhere:
life.

SEAGULL

Gabriel I angel am
cursed at sea
and cursed at land.

Blessed be the albatross
who with cold and rheumy eye
surveys his stormy citadel,
uncrowned neptunal king.

Blessed be the backbird's name,
his spectral scarecrow croak,
tending cornfield crop
on red and darkened wing.

But
Gabriel I angel am
cursed at sea
and cursed at land.

I nest upon the sea-kissed shore
and dream of albatross and blackbird—
oceans blasting forth from bays
fields rife with shooting stalks.

FIJI

When I was a child,
I speared tidal pools
with my eyes,
waded through coral castles,
flushed out eels,
scattered ink dot patterns
formed by schools of fish.

I would stare
at the trees blossoming
blood-red over the sea road.
Dying in allergies of beauty:
a cough, a wheeze,
a strangled choke.
Pollen and phlegm stained my lips.
The sea was distant then.

Once,
a striped Spanish Dancer,
a living skirt of jellied flesh,
washed up against the shore.
A girl and I found it
and buried its breaths in sand.
We did not think to set it free,
to throw it back
into the ebb-flow tides.

At night, the sun set
like a sheet of flame
over the waves,

purged the hours in fire
until even the ashes
had fallen from the sky.

THE PIGS OF GUINEA

dance upon white-surf waves
ride ghost bubbles from the sea,
skin shimmering like silver doubloons,
reflecting the wise-sly, old-new moon.

And the pigs of Guinea weave
their weird tales from palm fronds,
tell sailors' fortunes from
the gleam in storm-tossed eyes,
the rolling egg white of greed.

Until, finally, he who genuflects,
dripping whiting and grunion,
leaves the sky, gives way to
the mother-mistress,
the sun.

The pigs of Guinea slink
from the scorcher, this friend
to mad dog Englishmen.
For they are vain porkers—
the light burns them brown,
reveals age blotches on the old.

Blotches of sun say the foolish,
reliving legends of pygmies,
swine turned to stone like trolls,
moon-drinkers and sleep-stealers
no more; tired tusks root the ground,
seek sanctuary in dirt.

Thus they hide their hairy hides,
waiting for the slap-pounding surf,
for the glide and drift, the dance
of waves: where days end and myths
begin as bedtime stories.

And now, finally, the child sleeps.

TREES AND HOUSES

i.

The man whose eyes
pool around wrinkle deltas
stares out the window.
Houseshouses
and treestrees
blur by—
the bus moves
so fast.

A scowl.
Are the trees
among the houses
or the houses
among the trees?

ii.

Home now,
groceries forgotten
he putters
with his orchids,
eyes better focused
on detail,
a blade of finesse.

He lets his daughter
play near the edge

of the frog-throbbing lake,
near the edge of alligator jaws
and the strange gurgle
where earth meets water.

An orchid blade
pricks his finger
and he remembers
the bus, the trees, the houses.

He remembers
that houses are made of wood
and all the world's a forest.

His daughter becomes
his orchids, and he calls
her inside the tree of their house.
They eat and talk around
a wooden table.

Later,
though flesh
has fallen
from the bone
and his face is a ruin,
the mouth still smiles
and his gaze darts—
into the deep
and languished night,
among the trees,
unafraid of what they know.

SENTINELS

Fruit in buckets
and buckets round our waists,
we labor, bruising flesh blue,
eating the overripe with hungry mouths.

We talk across bushes,
between branches.
I joke that you are
the black-haired woman
of Blueberry Wood,
a new wave nymph
in shorts and T-shirt.

You say I must be
a foolish juggler of fruit.

Later, stomachs
and pails satisfied,
we leave the farm,
head out into the unknown,
past tombstones and honey hives,
thigh-high grass cutting our legs.

Our tongues slip
and slide
around their subject.
No branches to hide us,
just this wariness
beneath the skin.

FOUR THEORIES OF EARTH- MOON SYSTEM FORMATION

I. Fission

Boiling
  spinning
      down the black back
      alleys of space,
      raging through the cosmos,
      through constellations
      as yet unnamed . . .
      Earth and Moon entwined,
      tissues groaning in the push
      and pull, fighting invisible forces,
      attracting opposites
      split-split-

ting apart,
joined by threads
of natural law.

            – Moon rocks are
            chemically dissimilar
            from Earth rocks –

II. Capture

Spiraling masses
  hot-orphaned,
      Earth revolving
        round
        the
      sun of creation,
pockmarked Moon enticed,
attracted bodies drawn
to the point of mutual destruction.
The Moon forms an opal
over the churning Earth,
before both settle down
into watchful contemplation:
this silver eye, this red eye.

While the stars
revolve in perfect order,
as though they did not care
if life rose or crept
back into pools to die.

            – The Moon's orbit
            is circular rather
            than hyperbolic –

            III. Coeval

Masses twinning,
spawned from dust
into which they will return,
side by side:

the Man in the Moon
leering at the Woman
lost in the seas of Earth,
tossing her swirled hair,
blue-white reflection.

Sunspots float
like blossoming flowers,
decaying while these two
attracted lovers cover
the distance with longing,
gazes caught forever
by the memory-trap of dust,
creation; turning over
in sleep, fear is eclipsed
by solid rock.

> – *Why* are Moon
> rock different
> from Earth rocks? –

IV. Intervention

From the space
between spaces,
engines throb
        cough: drums heard underwater;
        the ship drags its body
        through the Dark with the fluid
        rigidity of made things.

The Moon,
chained behind,

teeter-totters forward,
tractor beams pulling.
Its seas are scooped out,
sucked dry of treasure.

The dreadnaught's engines
flare and cough and die,
Moon thrust into orbit
around a planet whose land quakes,
whose seas erupt with lava.
Celestial refuse flung into
the backwater . . .

              – How did
              the Earth-Moon
              system form? –

AN AFTERLIFE

White shatters blue.
Light rushes over plains,
across seas, between mountains.
Each night, stars flare and burn,
weeping fire, consumed.
The silence spreads and grows,
seeking every dark
and hidden place.

Yet still there is the after-
life, the glow of bone and flesh
in metal, ten faces waking
to the rising sun, so that
Time flows awry:
a day is a century,
a century a day.

> The wind blows east, through deserts
> and dim-lit plains, across swollen rivers
> and savannahs, reaching with dusty hands.

I. The Pauper of Ayutthya

Buddha reclines
crumbling in clay-green ruins.
(Ayutthya: city of kings,
Siam's sovereign capital
when the East rose like a beggar
from the streets of the world.)

Simple lines define features
worn down, eyes faint,
mouth a quiver.

Lost within himself,
the statue in repose
dreams still; he would not rise
should the world truly end.

Soon the jungle
will smother
his composure,
but a smile
will remain,
hidden by forest
camouflage.

> the wind travels past pungent Samarkand,
> through mountain passes, riding the Straits
> up into Istanbul, into Europe

II. The Paris Intellectual

A ramshackle mass of metal,
parasols forever ripped from hands,
buildings wrenched from street moorings.

Archaic arches have failed Rodin's Thinker,
carried him roughly to his final resting place.
He has pondered questions nightly
from atop the gates of Hell,
striven for truth even as it
rips the world apart.

He remembers the touch of human hands,
thinks in stasis, feels in statis,
bronze skin stagnant.
Tortured eyes survey the ruins
of the Four Horsemen,
brethren lying broken
round the Thinker in a mosaic
of scattered wood and marble.

Outside, trees wither.
Leaves spiral
in circles
to the ground.

    hiatus south,
    to the homeland
    of the Western heart:
    across mountains,
    down foothills,
    following paths
    to alabaster columns
    and azure skies;
    where gods are estranged
    and flesh has died,
    Olympus rules again.

III. Poseidon of the Frozen Metal Eyes

A windswept fortress,
the Acropolis
braves the sea
and Persia's haughty stare.

Poseidon gazes across the water,
body clothed in sea-green bronze,
arms caught in the motion of throwing a spear.
His eyes have been stripped,
leaving blankness
where once Pan and Artemis
came together in mad joy.

He dreams of freedom in the waves,
joining dolphins as they knife
through water, though he would drown
if he pulled his body seaward.

Behind him,
trapped in Acropolis columns,
korai smile wry idiot smiles
through marble locks.
Stone-etched memories,
they would weep if they could,
tears to fill the Aegean.
The statues stare at one another
in perfect longing,
men and women old in youth.

Only the sea's relentless chorus—
calling to the marble,
rushing up the steps—
will free them.

    south,
    across a sea
    still boiling
    from explosion

to Egypt,
where Seth and Osiris
claim the souls
of sunglazed peoples

IV. Cairo's Sphinx

Half-
human,
half-cat:
geometry,
ceremony,
death
wrapped together
in stone.

Wind-prey,
the Sphinx
locked to shifting sands
still murmurs to itself
as it has for forty centuries.
Life: a pinprick to its stone,
a momentary shiver;
eyes of dust, sweat,
and old god's visions.

> southwest, across the Atlantic, white-capped waves
> curling into themselves; Yucatan stands red
> in greeting, sunset curving through the sky

V. The Eyes of Chichen Itza

Sacrificial altars, stone ends
fashioned into heads, smiles breaking
compassion in cruelty:
Their feral friend, blood,
no longer trickles
down backs grooved
with dried wine.

Need intertwined
with their makers',
they discovered
the cutting edge of death
when Spanish boots
met New World sand.

Night comes to the
Plain of a Thousand Pillars.
Clever gargoyles
drink their own fear,
eyes watching
in the dark.

    north at daybreak, following the East Coast,
    skeletal crowds, ivory scattered,
    eternal traffic jams clogging streets—
    silence broken only by the rasps of dead rats

VI. The Lady of the Lamp

A harbor and a statue,
arms corroded, torch unlit,

listening to an underlying hum,
a phantom vibration
as her eyes welcome
ghosts from across
the ocean—shadow ships
with shadow captains
and shadow crews
endlessly reliving life.

The sounds of her country
siphoned through churches
and concrete and shopping malls,
but remembering nothing.

> west and south—seeking paths
> set by papyrus rafts:
> nightfall on a volcanic island
> where sunset burns—
> a plunging amber blade

VII. Star-Charted Easter Island

Shadow mimics stone,
noses cleft from living rock
Buried in the ground, chins
slide to subterranean necks.
Statues chiseled
as sculptors died
of disease, joined
ancestors in the star-charted sky.

Slanted eyes linger on the tide,
the passage of sea turtles,

burrowing into sand, laying eggs,
lumbering back into the waves,
water washing over them.

They remember outriggers
and brown-skinned people,
muskets downing thrushes,
blood from crimson throats.

They dream of houses open
to the nightly sprawl of galaxies,
island home and host.

> west still farther, following
> sea sargasso trails, tasting salt;
> moving overland to the ocean,
> reaching toward an island
> where caverns wait,
> water drip-
> dripping.

VIII. Siva of the Elephanta Caves

Crushed under the weight of stone,
Lord Siva lies imprisoned
within a wall, carved in high relief;
double-jeweled crowns ring his head.
God of Destruction and Renewal,
his eyes could form and unform
the universe in a single blink.

Nothing has ever held him
from his tasks—

not Alexander
not Moghuls
not the Europeans.

Always, his four arms open to invaders,
he swallows them.

    northwest—
    a wrenching dislocation,
    faster than the wind,
    half-way round the world
    to Rome
    to Romulus, to Remus,
    to the centurion astride his stallion.

IX. The Fallen Soldier

Eyes stare from beaten bronze,
features sallow, skin yellow
if born of flesh, parchment drawn
taut, old and tearing.
Broken teeth shine from his mouth.
Hair curls like serpents about his brow.

A flame still burns within his frame.
He remembers frenzy in hot forges,
blacksmith's curses, the clank of weapons,
the grind of bit and harness.

Forever standing still,
he leads charges into battle,
a soldier spending
lives and light.

Hollow, surrounded by death,
he hisses, "Rome lives!"
inside his metal skull.

fragmenting to any of a hundred churches,
any of a hundred alcoves burnt and broken,
priests gone, halls empty,
religion's place usurped

X. The Angel by the Altar

Ringed by a garden of ash,
marble cherubim sing
within chapel walls.

A wooden child
stands by the altar,
wings charred,
feet blackened by soot.

The child's hands are bound
in pristine symmetry.
Not Dante himself
nor the Thinker's
Four Horsemen
could wrench
a confession
from him.

```
            *
            *
            *
        NORTH


*  *  * WEST        *         EAST *  *  *


        SOUTH

            *

            *

            *
```

The wind
bites deep;
the world consumes
images creatures
once raised to depict themselves—
seeking company in solitude,
light in darkness.

Dust
and sand
and a few statues
to defy time,
defy time
again.

THE SHIP AT THE EDGE OF THE WORLD

Grounded at the world's edge,
waiting for rescue
that will not come—
we need only cast our gaze
toward other ships caught,
the tangled metal of breached hulls,
the main sails snapped,
ragged flags aflutter,
drowned in the current.

We came here to prove the world
is round, enraptured
with the details of discovery,
to discover too late the truth,
and now sit balanced
upon the final, tottering line
that separates sea from
land sea from sky sea
from the downward rush
of stars and years.

Of first mate, coxswain, cook,
riggers, sailors, swabbers,
only the captain stood undismayed
upon the prow, balanced Adonis-like
against the huge, occluded eye
of the sun.

And when he jumped, he jumped
like a lover like a diver
like dolphin,
not in dishonor, disdain or failure,
but glorious.

And when we rushing to the rail
looked down hundreds, thousands
of feet, our gaze tumbling
down, there he was: pale body
against the sun, moon, stars,
not plummeting, no not
plummeting but gliding
down.

While the rest of us
embrace neither life
nor death, but linger here
in the seasons of the sun
in the seasons of the moon,
in darkness and in light.

We watch the seagulls laugh
of their escape,
watch the white water foam,
listen to the creak of timbers
like brittle muscles,
and wonder when we
will no longer have
a choice.

FICTION

THE SONGS
A DEAD WHALE SINGS

The sea spawned the whale and, ultimately, the sea left the whale upon the shore, along with a tangle of beer bottles, plastic wrappers, tar-coated sargasso weed, used rubbers, and soft drink cans. No one could determine the whale's species; to each spectator, the whale took on the characteristics of the breed most harped upon: nar or white, blue or beluga. The eyes were large and liquid, the skin beginning to dry, the great jaws half-open.

Despite the flies, despite the heat, despite the rising stench of rotted flesh, a crowd gathered around the leviathan. They poked it. They prodded it. Some enterprising soul even cut a memento from the flukes with a penknife. Children, free of any moral constraints, scrambled atop the vast, white midsection and danced on the skin and, where exposed, the flesh. The whale did not see the indiscretion, for a New Jersey pickle manufacturer had already plucked the eyes from the hoary face and plopped them in a jar, to ferment as delicacies for jaded Chinese bureaucrats. Then a lumberjack on holiday brought his chainsaw down from his truck and, with a whir of aggression that belied his four-foot-nine height and beanpole arms, he began to slice the whale into fleshy two-by-four's.

Soon the belly opened—breached with a snorted pock-push sound—and an "ohhh . . . " arose from the crowd. For within the belly lay moist treasures beyond number. The lumberjack was the first to enter and, upon observing that no awful fate had befallen him, the crowd surged into the gap, into the fleshy cavern. Even the children stopped their dance and formed a necklace of hands, giggles, and motion that flowed into the belly. The lead child found a cat's skeleton and they promptly twirled out again, content to play pick-up-bones in the sand. As for the adults, it was a mad scramble to claim the remaining contents. The lumberjack snatched a damp volume, read the spine, and threw it away. A copy of the communist manifesto—common in the bellies of deep-water fish, now that so many countries had tossed their copies into the sea. But other books were caught in the stomach's lining, priceless special editions of Edward Whittemore's *Jerusalem Poker*, Amanda Manichikan's *A Tirade of Clowns*, Phillips' *The God of Comedy*, and a thousand more besides, smelling of seaweed, damp but readable. An unhealthy diet of the macabre and the humorous, combined without regard for propriety.

One old man was heard to remark that he'd never seen a whale so well read. But an English woman scoffed, saying: A man might have lived in this place for a time, or perhaps the whale swallowed a library, but anything it learned was surely secondhand, and meant nothing to its aqueous brain. Surely it could not read, nor do arithmetic. It had no opposable thumb to stick in jam or signal a cab or plug a dike or tickle a baby's belly. It had no thoughts but peculiar wet dreams within that skull of water . . . No one could contradict her, for the New Jersey pickler had already stolen the brain. Instead, they began to catalog the belly's contents: a black, frayed butterfly net, a cross on a chain (simple, such as a priest might wear), a barely readable poster proclaiming the "Sparks Circus," a large water jug (a shriveled, ether-preserved arm floating within it), a barnacle-encrusted M-16, two jeweled frogs made of jade, three million krill, seven miles of fishing line, eight hundred square feet of fishing net, one ton of plastic bags.

The old man pondered aloud on the wisdom of a whale that could entertain such a diverse collection of oddities, but the English woman ignored him this time. The krill, line, net, and bags were left behind, but the other items did not remain in the whale's stomach for long.

The sun beat down.

The heat fried the sweat on people's skin.

The sand took on a reddish sheen.

At first, the arguments over who would take which treasures were quite urbane, but fights soon broke out, resulting in bloodied noses and a few sprained opposable thumbs. These skirmishes grew into battles, then wars, split along ethic and religious lines. Now faces were punched, spleens kicked, knees cracked by baseball bats. The shouts of haggling became constant screams. When one ended—a banshee, a raw nerve end—another began—a yodeler, a beast shrieking—only to be cut off by a strangled hiss or choke.

The M-16 had live ammunition, and the lumberjack, suddenly six-foot-five with arms as thick as the trees he cut, sprayed them all with the awful sharp agony of bullets. The children played on in the bones, eating the gristle, the marrow. Soon the war engulfed the shiny, shellacked beach houses, the pale, baby-blue artifices set among the dunes, the reeds, so that only the roofs raised like ships' prows, surreal and monstrously out of place, above the sea of bushes, sand, and grass. Now the treasures were viscera, steaming livers culled from unwilling bodies—and stomachs, pulled purpling from distended bellies; for if a fish could hide such beauties, what marvels within the bread basket of the human form?

While the blinded whale looked on, the sun outlining the imperfections of the skin, the pockmarked ripples that spoke of travels from Australia to Antarctica, through the deep blue hardness of the cold, through the streamlined mask of water; the scars upon the flukes that remembered high and surging breaches, the uplifting from the water that signified a whale might fly, if only for a moment. That signified the songs a dead whale sings.

THE FLOWER VENDOR

If you follow the path of the hat back from where it blows across the sidewalk, tattered and abandoned, you will discover the owner: a dead man in the street. He wears a dirty T-shirt and dirtier brown jacket over the T-shirt. His badly bleached jeans are torn from constant wear. The man, whose name is Stretcher Jones (it says so on his T-shirt: "I am Stretcher Jones and I Love the Truth") stares up at the sky. The sky has a stretched quality to it, a balloon blown so big that the blue has been bleached to a grainy off-white.

Stretcher Jones is gaunt beneath his jeans. Sprawled on the concrete, half in, half out of the gutter, he might as well be a load of firewood, all a-kilter and askew. You stand over him, note the eyes that seem only a reflection of the sky, the dry heat, the blue strung out and washed away by repetition.

A stretcher, you say to the people who pass him on the street. A stretcher for Stretcher Jones. But, like the gray and sleek sharks in the downtown aquarium that must endlessly swim forward or drown, the people keep walking, walking to work amid the *endless*, the *always*, the *never* sound of watches—time inflated to individual ticks that well up in a squall of minutes, seconds, milliseconds.

First and second hands hold no meaning for Stretcher Jones; he hangs always between one tick and the next.

Anymore. Someday. Everywhen.

Stretcher Jones appears calm to you, despite the red dot that punctuates the T-shirt, smack in the center of the "c" in "Stretcher". He no longer notices the woman sobbing in the barbershop doorway. Or the man with features like the swift strokes of Japanese letters, the man who is walking away from Stretcher Jones, a smoking gun in his left hand. He has been walking away for thirty minutes and he always ends up in mid-step outside the barbershop, intending to walk away thirty minutes more and yet remain where he is.

Was. Will be. Will always be.

Next to Stretcher Jones' curling cold hand lies a cracked vase full of roses as red as arterial blood. In the dryness, they smell like passion, like betrayal. You notice that the woman wears a rose fastened to her dress, just above her left breast. She wears a ring on her right hand, as does the man with the gun. Stretcher Jones wears only his calm expression, his dirty clothes—the T-shirt that reads, "I am Stretcher Jones and I Love the Truth."

It rains minutes now, their stinging touch tap-tap-tapping your temples.

You pick up the hat, rescuing it from the ever-forward clatter of shoes, and dust it off. You straighten the brim. You tap it against your thigh. There are no holes in it. True, it is tattered, but this lends it a world-weariness that appeals to you.

You leave the clothes for someone else, but you take the hat, and then you move on, rejoin the other walkers.

After all, the body, the woman, the man, are not part of your story and you, unlike Stretcher Jones, cannot always love the truth.

Sometimes you hate the truth.

THE COUNTY FAIR

There! There! The roulette wheel in the sky. You are
     there. The county fair. The ferrous revolves and you spin and
topple with it. This is the place you cannot fail to lose
     your money
     your state of mind.
     You enter timid, small, alone; you cannot help but notice the
rhythm of
     the crowds
     the clanging machinery
     the fly-plagued animals
     Cannot help but find the rhythm invading your skin, your
flesh, the bones beneath, the very marrow. The wet grass mixed
with smoke. The *kush* of cotton candy against your mouth.
Shirtsleeve against shirtsleeve. The silhouette of a giraffe
chained behind a fence, the huddled capybara, musky fur cross-
cut by the wire cage. The couple French-kissing beneath the jug-
gernaut roller coaster. Guess your weight. Guess your age. Take
a ride. Guess your wait. Read your palm. So many palms—
pressed to pockets, joined, at sides. A world of appendages,
conversing among themselves. Your pulse races as the wheel
turns; you dip low, recover.

You enter timid, small, alone; you cannot help but notice
the hastily erected tents
the monstrous tire tracks of trucks.
You can navigate around them, avoid the mud. But
a maze remains; people fat thin pear-shaped oblong asym-
metrical. Corridors to freedom formed by fatty's tush, bulgy's
breasts. Come. Come on by, see if you can get through without
the big
SQUASH.

And, when you have found.
When you have found.
Found.
The center, there you are with your money. Money. You left it
in your pocket; you can feel it: coiled, waiting, restless.
When you have found the game stall.

This stall has always appeared for you, others like you, as
you move liquidly through the moment.
You enter timid, small, alone; you cannot help but notice
green budgies, blue bears hang from the walls. Plastic bowie
knives. Flags. False fur, eyes eyes staring from the walls. All
those eyes. You cannot believe your
eyes.
There! There! The Ferris wheel. And you, under its spell,
must have
HAVE
the bear. The brilliant bright beautiful bear waiting just for
you. You may still be alone. You may have picked up a friend
or two. It does not matter.
Dollar a shot. Dollar a shot. Balloons. Darts.
Hit. The Balloons. Concentrate . . . Aim. And. Hit. Them.
POP. Each breakage brings you closer to the prize. The wheel is

a mandala inside your head. You are (money) so far (you arrived timid) outside your (tush and breasts) mind.

The man. The man behind the counter. The man behind the counter with no eyes. Correction. A mirror for a left eye, a clock for the right. A crooked line of mouth. A pout. A smile. A smirk.

Tick. Tock. Tick. He laughs with his clock, his mirror eyes. You see your face in that eye, distorted, squished and slug-like. The man is rushing you, forcing your dollars onto the counter. Against your will: you who broke through the maze, tore your eyes, bleeding, from the wheel.

The man has teeth. Many rows of teeth, in places where no teeth should be. You don't care. You don't care that no one else brushes against you in this darkness, that you are somehow on the fair's outskirts. You don't care because

YOU WANT THAT BEAR. You don't know why. The man laughs harder, with his mouth. YOU WANT THAT BEAR. The bills flutter from your hands like doves. Green, greasy doves.

But:

closer to the bear.

Closer. Closer. Dart. Balloon. Pop. There! You have won a plastic thingee. *A plas tick thing gee.* You have no use for it, cannot guess its function beyond the obscene, but you have won it. Onward. Ever onward. (How many? How many darts have you thrown without paying?) Blind. Blind. The man has blinded you with the mirror in his eye.

Twelve darts. Thirteen. Fourteen. Give me more. Give me. What use is the light, the warmth, the love you do not have and cannot get? *Give me more.*

(Out of sight, across the ropes, the lines, the mud, the capybara in its pen laughs through the dust on its lungs. "O man, O man," it softly moans. "I had shape once. I had shape. Now I am nothing. All for the dream. The dream of blue bears . . . ")

Too late. Too late. The wheel has come around again.

-nth dart. Hit! Hit! Homerun. Touchdown. You win.

And there is your bear. There! The bear.

YOUR BEAR.

A blue teddy bear that

UP CLOSE

has seen too many miles. Too many miles. A spackle of dust accusing as bloodstains.

The green greasy faces of Jefferson, Grant, Washington have deserted you. The man behind the counter puts out a hand. Pay up. Pay up. You cannot hide in the human maze. It has disappeared.

Ten.

Only darkness. Only the moan of trucks and other beasts. Only the wind threading through trees, the smoke, the moist grass treacherous underfoot. *Only your own loneliness like a flat, smooth stone across your belly.*

Nine.

The man's face (*you knew this before*) is overgrown (*but only now has*) with teeth (*the fear set in*). The wheel dips down with a smile. The lights flash over you. No sound. No sound. Just nomoney your nomoney jackknife heartbeat.

Eight.

Too many darts. Too many balloons.

Seven.

The man's teeth grind and clash. You run. Run. Your feet are anvils. The teeth pursue. Frictionless. Fast. Don't.

Six.

Don't look back. The red moon pins you down. Where are all the people. Where? And where is the man?

Five.

There!

Four.
Fangs cut the air.
Three.
There! Don't.
Two.
Cut flesh.
One.
You are
broke.
You are
broken.

O Capybara, King Capybara, sing a song. As the wheel
turns. Under the august moon. Of greed. Of blue bears. The
county fair. *You came timid, small, alone;*

    you could not help but notice
    notice the new cage
    the new cage that contains you
    contains your soul
    your soul in the body
    the body of a capybara

    because you have no money
    no money can repay
    repay them for your greed
    your greed at the county fair
    county fair—there
    there don't cry
    cry.

KAERU

Wind-ruffled cherry blossoms glided to earth, some coming to rest in the Princess' lap. Their touch brought her from meditation to a sleepy self-awareness.

She raised her head, squinting into the sun, which had dipped to the horizon, its rays tangled in the branches of the cherry trees, its reflection rippling across the pond. Behind her, she could hear a low buzz of voices; the palace and loyal court awaited her command.

The Princess ignored them, eyes wandering over the water. Petals dotted the pond—and strider insects, skittering along as if on stilts. She concentrated on the sharp ripples of their wake and smiled, meditation fully broken.

A larger ripple caught her attention. A frog surfaced amid the floating petals. The Princess's jet eyes opened wide in astonishment. The frog stared at her, then swam to the bank.

"Long life," it croaked.

"Long life," the Princess replied. "But there are no frogs in the gardens. Nor is it the natural order of things that frogs should talk."

The frog clambered out of the water, hopping onto the dais. Its back glistened with droplets and its feet were crowned with gold. The frog fixed its gaze upon her.

"Many pardons, Princess, but the natural order has been broken. The old ways die."

The Princess raised her eyebrows. She wondered if this creature was an Elder, come from the dead to test her. "How can this be true?" She gestured toward the garden. "Everything is as it should be, except for you, frog."

"Is it, Princess?" replied the frog. He turned to face the west. "It will be night soon and still the petals fall."

The Princess laughed, jewels tinkling on her arms and legs. " 'Into the old pond a frog suddenly plunges; the sound of water.' You are a writer of riddles, frog! Tell me what you mean."

The frog watched the fading sun. "Princess, I do not know how to tell you except in halves. Something moves in my skin. A petal struck me and I burned."

"Perhaps your skin is too sensitive," the Princess said playfully.

The frog shook its head, its whole body saying no. "My skin is thick, set in layers like the oak. I am old. My skin does not burn easily. I tell you, my child, I feel change."

"Please," said the Princess. "Do not call me a child. I sit here for long hours, meditating in my garden. I know something of the world."

The frog shivered and did not reply. He saw doves trembling on the cherry trees, their silhouettes rough against the chill. A wind had risen from the west; branches swayed in the darkening sky. The sun had disappeared and the gardens, from willows to plum trees, gardenias to snapdragons, were painted a shade of slate.

Presently, a servant girl padded up on cat feet and murmured in the Princess' ear.

"No," she whispered. "Send them away. Send everyone

away for tonight." The servant girl bowed low and was gone.

Turning to the frog, the Princess said, "Is there danger? Where does the danger come from?"

The frog's eyes glistened in the dark. "Pardon, Princess, but I said 'change,' a change strong enough to burn my skin."

She laughed. "Change is dangerous. My father the Emperor has taught me that. Now, tell me, how may I discover the nature of this change for myself?" She bowed to the frog, her raven hair falling in waves about her face. "For what other reason have you been sent, other than to guide me or test me."

"You do me honor," the frog said, bowing in his turn. "My skin tells me, 'Seek out a high place.' Perhaps then we may find an answer."

The Princess nodded. "We shall go to the Tower of the Winds."

And so the Princess walked through the shadow lands of the gardens, the frog nestled in her hands. The touch burned the frog's skin, but he did not cry out.

Ringed by willow trees, the Tower of the Winds lay at the center of the gardens. It tunneled into the sky, crown lost in darkness, pagoda wings outstretched. The door stood open, petals strewn across the threshold. The Princess stared at the massive turret, up past clouds to where the moon and stars lay masked. She hesitated, then entered the tower, her sandals slipping against stone.

"May the steps be short," muttered the frog, eyes shut against the drumming pain of her hands, forelegs locked in prayer. As they ascended the spiraling stairway, the Princess could see, through windows cut into the walls, the ground receding and, to the East, palace torches guttering as the servants made ready for bed. She climbed the last set of steps and, breathing heavily, stumbled out onto the roofed crown.

"Oh," she said in surprise. She let the frog hop from her hands onto the protecting wall. "Oh," she said again. And then, "Ohm." The Princess brought her hands to her mouth. Flames rose in the west, reflected in the frog's eyes.

"This is the change, Princess."

Under the pitch sky, beyond the gardens' invisible walls, in the foothills of the Emperor's lands, a battle had been joined. To the Princess, this battle was only a canopy of light through which brighter flashes streaked. But she had read the old tales: stories of entire wars fought beneath cover of darkness, of the Army-That-Casts-No-Shadow. Her heart beat like a thousand rice sparrow wings and her hands fluttered with it. She flinched as if receiving a blow.

"I can see the men, my Princess," said the frog, whose senses had ripened with age. "They have blackened faces. Many stumble or fall. Spiked wheels crush them. Catapults fling hot oil on them. Wizards let loose their spores, the weapons that sniff out flesh like sharks and burrow like maggots. The lines, they shift like 'the sea at springtime: all day it rises and falls, yes, rises and falls.' But I think, I believe, the invaders press forward."

"Change," said the Princess, "is dangerous."

She repeated this sentence as if it were a mantra, a balm for her troubled mind. The wind brought her the oily scent of smoke, the clash of sword on sword.

" 'You summer grasses!' " quoted the frog in a lean, strong voice. " 'Glorious dreams of great warriors, now only ruins.' "

The Princess raised her head, looked at the frog. "It is not possible. He has not told me this. He would have told me this." Her eyes shone with anger and her face tightened with the beginnings of fear.

"Everything is as it should be, Princess," the frog

reminded her. "But there must always be time for a person to face the change. Your father has neglected this responsibility."

The Princess scarcely heard, for she leaned against the wall, her eyes wet as she looked out on the slowly-nearing battle. The frog felt the heat of her against his skin, saw the corona surrounding her. The Princess was awash with flames. And within the fire only he could comprehend, the frog saw her beauty with all of his age-old senses, her hair caught by the wind, her skin alabaster-smooth, and shallow.

"Who are they?" she asked.

"The invaders? Why, Princess, they are your own gardener, your own maid, or people like them. Your father has been an unwise ruler."

The Princess brought up her hand to strike the frog, the bells at her wrists jingling harshly, but halted on the downward motion. She stiffened as she turned away from him, stood straight. Below, the fires hunched their slow way to her garden walls. Somewhere, a nightingale burst into song.

" 'When a thing is said, the lips become very cold, like the autumn wind.' "

"Do not quote ghosts." The Princess's voice held a hint of winter frost.

"Sometimes the words of our Elders . . . "

She spun around, voice loud and shrill. "Do not preach to me, or I will talk to you in the language of the dead: 'The little rain frog rides on a banana tree as it softly sways.' Be careful you do not fall!"

The frog's body quivered. "Sometimes, the words of our Elders hold much that is wise to repeat . . . little rain frog."

The frog looked at her, saw only flames, while the Princess stared into his eyes, rimmed with reflected light, and saw that they were scarred with pain.

The Princess's breath left her in a rush, her shoulders sagged.

Head down, she approached the frog. "Forgive me, Elder. I know you test me."

"I have not said I was an Elder," said the frog. "But I accept your regret—and your pain. We must always respect our fathers. But now I must tell you how the world works outside of your gardens. And if at daybreak we find the armies have moved far from here, you must still remember what I tell you."

The bitterness in her mouth, the heightened smell of attar, caused the Princess's eyes to tear as the frog spoke.

"I shall tell you why the petals fall and why the trees shall bear much fruit this spring," the frog said, his voice rising and falling. "Your father the Emperor has caused the world to collapse around him. He has killed without justice in his heart."

The frog's voice formed a list and litany, containing the bones of all the dead, the grief of the wronged, the hunger of the poor. "He has taken rice from the destitute." The gaunt haikus dropped from his mouth until the Princess understood that there must be a sharing of the blame. "He has jailed artisans who worked with the sacred images."

With each new charge, the Princess winced, but said nothing. Her silence masked pain as the frog told her of beggars huddled in the cities, the secret death courts, the judges jaundiced by corruption, the farmers driven from their livelihoods, the families thrown out of their houses by the Emperor's troops.

When the frog had finished, his voice a whisper of its former self, dry and exhausted, the Princess wept for her father, who had kept these things from her. She cried for the thousands condemned to poverty while she meditated in her garden of delights.

And when she had wiped the last tear from her face, the nightingale's melody twinned to her sobs, the sun began its ascension. And when she stared down from the tower, she saw that the trees were bare. The world had come to her. The rebels were at the palace gates, their cries of victory rising above the din of struggle. Their numbers darkened the hills: a wave breaking upon her gardens. Faces like pale moons jostled one another as they pressed forward, through the smoldering gates. She searched in vain for her father's banner.

Voice masking sadness, the frog said, "The rebels will come here. What will you do?"

"What can I do?" the Princess replied. "There is a change upon the world. I am of the old, by my father's design."

Her incisive gaze pinned him. "Who are you? Tell me, please, before . . . " She gestured at the army below, which was now pouring through the palace doors and windows in a flood, drowning the red-and-black livery of the Emperor's personal guard, but not quite drowning their screams.

"I am your Ancestor, great great grand-daughter. I once ruled over all of these lands with neither success nor failure. I was advisor to myself and took too little advice."

The Princess pressed her palms together. "I am named Bright Camilia." She laughed, an edge of self-mockery entering her voice. "It has been enlightening, Ancestor. If you had not spent so much time talking, I might have escaped."

Hands shaking, she swung herself onto the wall and sat there, legs dangling over the side. She gazed down. The flood had reached the tower and crashed onward; already, she could hear people on the staircase. She turned to the frog, inclined her head, and jumped. The Elder saw only a flame—a flame that spun as it dropped, extinguished as it hit the river of people below. Her body vanished, trampled into the earth of her garden.

" 'Falling upon earth, pure water spills from the cup of the camilia,' " he said, the pages of a book turning in his mind. His skin no longer burned, but his heart was cold, as though winter had already arrived. The steps behind him rang with the hollow sound of boots.

The five haikus included in the story are by, in order of appearance, Basho, Buson, Basho, Kikaku, and Basho.

A SOCIAL GATHERING

Rubber tires tearing—screech of cars knowing they will hit, an instant of silence pounding eardrums, impact a dull crunching thud. X marks the spot, crumpled carcasses glittering at the intersection's center. For a moment, the scene is an impressionist painting, joggers caught in mid-step, traffic immobile. Vultures halt in the jet stream, which thickens to molasses. Then a cricket orchestra strikes a dirge, a turgid twister of sound. Metal gleams coppery-bronze in the late afternoon sun and people come awake. A cop, passing by on his way home to dinner, parks his car, gets out, assesses damage, makes a report, speaking with superiors about traffic control logistics.

The participants in this event emerge from their vehicles, scratching heads, kicking at tires. Some stagger, perhaps giddy from impact. Journeyman girl watchers, dog walkers, mobile talkers, congregate around the intersection. Neighbors slink from their homes to gossip like ghouls over the bones of disaster. Dents are inspected yet again, *ohs* and *ahs* rising over the resumed rumble of cars. Somewhere, a condemned murderer laughs. An opinionated female stripper, head attacked by curlers, tells the officer, *I saw everything. The green car maliciously turned on a yellow light.* The green car, when questioned, denies all, its owner patting it on the hood, backing up his car's tale. A would-be driving instructor who lives in the corner house—the one built in the shape of a yellow submarine—takes notes, confers with the stripper. A fundamentalist with three nostrils whose home is festooned with American flags snorts and huffs and puffs and talks about acts of God, asking the red car to repent its communist ways and replace hammer and sickle with a scepter. Leaking oil, the red car declines this offer and dies on the spot, without confession.

As the crowd continues to gather, an ice cream truck pulls up, tooting its horn, smiling and playing "The Way We Were" on its speakers. Kids run to it from the nearby park. Soon a hot dog stand has joined it, shouting out the prices of its wares: *Two fah a dollah! Two fah a dollah!* A newspaper vendor clumps down the street, shrieks, *Accident on 34th Street: Car Dies in Bumper-Blender! Read all about it in me!* People pour in, as if to fit the mold of a giant hot cross bun. The news has gone out over the airwaves and highways: accident! Extended families of Italians passing through on their way to Miami picnic by the roadside. A group of socially aware punks spray-paints LOOSE BRUCE on the policeman's car while he interrogates drivers. Whether this means Bruce is behind bars and wants out or that he is simply promiscuous, no one can say. Certainly not the bag ladies who, with no transportation of their own, arrive by bus. Wealthy divorcees rent elegant limousines. The *ohs* and *ahs* continue, drowning out the other sounds.

Like the musical creak of swings in the nearby park. Like the *ummph!* of grass growing. Like the footfalls of unattended Great Danes pounding the pavement. Like the mockingbird that whistles Dixie, passed down from its great-great-to-the-nth-degree grandfather, who picked it up while marching with Sherman into Georgia. The park itself has decided to ignore the accident, an event that entices patrons away from its innate beauty.

But then a brother and sister collide (brother's fault) and sister falls from her bike, skinning nose, skinning toes, skinning pantyhose. *Good riddance on those ridiculous 'hose,* her mother says as she picks her daughter up. *They seemed to have a life of their own, making you wear lipstick and pop birth control pills—and you only eight.*

I didn't hear you. I did not see you, she says, accusing her brother. She sits down, but the grass protests, heaves her off their humming stalks. Perhaps she prepares for future car crashes, as a cub will stalk in play.

A portly man walking alongside a rottweiler takes the park's position and ignores the accident crowd. The rottweiler ignores even the girl who has skinned everything.

Back at the crash site, the policeman has accepted an invitation by the Italian family to visit their house, having fallen deeply in love with the family's grandmother, while the younger daughter has fallen for him. Her horoscope book sighs from her overflowing purse. It tells her a crash site is not romantic enough for a first meeting. She protests that statistics show crash sites are the best places for meeting single men, since they have the most crashes. The horoscope book shuts up, pages pouting.

By now, the tow trucks have arrived, sniffing around the site, looking for disabled cars, but are frustrated by the jumble of people. Disgusted, they give up, roar off after easier prey—like stranded Winnebagos.

Lights have been set up, streets cordoned off. The band has arrived. It plays heavy metal, country, R&B, and pop in a swelling tempo, to lyrics no one can understand. The park rolls over on its side and goes to sleep, displacing squirrels' nuts and hamstringing the evening joggers.

The crash couples have (apparently) forgiven each other and

are already arranging marriages between eligible bachelor-bachelorettes on both sides. Dances begin, informally as twitches and moonwalks, before coalescing into mambas, limbos, and waltzes. The bag ladies square dance with the bag gentlemen. The divorcees strut their stuff with house painters, chimney sweeps, and failed novelists. The female stripper, putting on a PG show, strips down to a blouse and shorts, eliciting gasps from the junior high boys who have formed a tight circle around her. The man with the three nostrils demonstrates picking his nose for interested passersby. No one is interested—except for the woman with the third eye. They hit it off. Only later, in bed, does the fundamentalist realize the woman is a transvestite.

Above, nighthawks trade weather reports while moths dive bomb bird nests, shouting *Che Guevara lives!* The night has a creamy texture to it, the sun doffing its hat and leaving for warmer parts. Lamps cast shades of vanilla light. Fires glow in barbecues brought to accommodate the party's gustatory needs. At midnight, the red car is buried in the intersection, as is the custom, its hood left showing as a memorial. Its grieving owner takes a memento: the left side mirror. The green car expresses its grief with a mournful toot of its horn. It decides to spend the night in the intersection and burrows beneath the blanket it brought along in case.

The fires bank. The wind picks up. The night cools. By twos and threes and fours and bakers' dozens, the celebrants disperse. The crash participants shake hands again and smile. The red car owner shares the bus with the bag people. The extra lights are repacked. The band gathers its instruments and leaves for Tucson and a five a.m. jam. Taxis escort the divorcees, some attended and others not, to their respective palatial dives. The Italian family ravels up its rolls of spaghetti, the policeman caught in the noodles, and departs for Miami. The hot dog stand heads off with the ice cream truck to a quiet gas station for some late night motor tuning. The newspaper vendor has been put to bed hours earlier.

Quiet becomes the order of the night. Serenity. The guerilla warfare between nighthawks and moths continues—but quietly, so as not to bring the pest control truck from its den. The park, startled by silence, wakes up and rolls back into position. The squirrels chatter byzantine curses.

Much later, the scuttling forms of insurance agents and their laptops tiptoe from shadow to shadow. They measure widths, cut off samples of this and that. They wear white gloves signed by Michael Jackson. They leave as craftily as they have come, computer screens blinking glassy-eyed with cost estimates. After they are gone, the muggers uncurl from grottos and put up "Safe Place" signs. They wait with net and gig for unwary children and necking teenagers.

Morning. Sunday. The sun has reappeared. The green car warms itself, ready to rev its engines and rejoin its owners. But what's this? Planes rip through the cloud banks, pamphlets falling from cargo holds in flocks of paper: lawsuit notices carried on gossamer wings, until the gossamer wearies and shakes them loose. Tiny parachutes open and float gently down to the intersection until it is snowing—Christmas in September! Lawsuits for everyone! The red car's memorial roof is covered and smothered. The green car yawns, signs, and starts the ignition. The accident has ended all too soon. It has a hangover.

A FEW NOTES UPON FINDING A GREEN ALIEN BABY FIGURINE IN A SPECIMEN TRAP AT LONGITUDE ___, LATITUDE ___, ANTARCTICA

Dr. Larry Gilchrist, Ph.D.

To be honest, my first thought as research leader was: *I'm not prepared for this.* Then the relief poured over me as Dave and Sandra pulled the object free of the trap and I understood it was plastic. It could not have been more plastic had "Made in China" been tattooed on its posterior. Still, something about its sightless eyes mocked me. I demanded Dave and Sandra explain its presence in the trap. For several weeks, I had begun to believe they doubted my abilities as research leader, a well-deserved promotion due to my twenty-two years of seniority. I was almost certain Dave resented it—and if Dave, then Sandra.

"How did it get in there?" I asked. The trap had been empty when I had sent it down through the hole in the ice, down into that endless dark blue penetrating the seamless white.

Dave shrugged, denied culpability. Sandra merely raised her

eyebrows. I could feel the heat of their disdain, but decided to ignore it. The walls of our "research station"—shack, hovel, tin-plated survival square, whatever you wish to call it—were more than usually claustrophobic.

"Where could it have come from?"

Unanswered, thwarted, my question hung in the air like our breath on those rare occasions now when we would venture outside to check the batteries on the snow mobile or to gauge the direction and strength of the Antarctic wind that can scorch the ears with its incessant moaning.

Where could it have come from? We manned Research Outpost #25, thirty miles from the main McMurdo Station base, and except for seals and single-celled plant organisms, a few fish burbling in deep thought beneath us, there were no other suspects.

"Maybe the last research team left it behind," Sandra suggested, too sensibly.

I thought I saw Dave smirk. I resented the insinuation that I hadn't checked the trap carefully the day before.

Sandra could not meet my gaze and began to check the trap for rips and tears, preparing to send it back into the lower depths.

The rest of the day was spent in a perfunctory silence and in taking minute measurements from the adjacent ice fields. Dave's instruments might as well have been of alien construction; I was pure biologist, he technophile, dependent on a wide range of tools for his job. I needed merely the evidence of my eyes and a certain cunning to intuit and improvise my profession.

And yet, I must admit, all day, well into false dusk, I could not shake the feeling of being watched. I would stare over at the plastic figurine and wonder if it analyzed me much as I analyzed seal shit or the mating call of the male royal penguin.

I am by nature a solitary person, and even when sharing an apartment with my girl friend a few years ago (a micro-biologist; for some reason, she didn't like it when I told people "yes—she's a tiny little person"), before we broke up (an argument about plant cells), I could not accustom myself to the presence of another human being. I had come to Antarctica to get away from people while still pursuing my rather ambitious career goals (startling discovery; Swedish honors). Alas, I had been assigned by a sadistic bureaucrat to be confined to a cramped space with individuals I was not fond of, all of us staring at a hole in the ice for the better part of four months. It was not everything I had thought it would be . . .

And now this. The alien baby made me uncomfortable, as if it had unbalanced the, dare I say, human equation. It took up space for all of its small size: the radiant green of its plasticized skin somehow amplified its presence. Its guileless smile, that idiot cleft of a grin, said it all. *Welcome to the end of your career*, it said. *Congratulations—you're going nowhere, fast.*

The next day, the situation worsened. The trap did not come back up. I stared at the broken metallic rope in my be-gloved hand in shock.

Again, Dave and Sandra were of little help.

"It could have frayed against the ice," Dave suggested.

"A narwhal or elephant seal might have been able to damage it," Sandra said.

I looked at them both as I would a couple of apes shitting from the upper branches of a baobab tree, circa 30,000 years ago.

"The ice didn't fray it," I said. "An elephant seal didn't cut it with its teeth. One of you sabotaged it."

David tried to protest. "Now, Larry, that's really not fair—"

"Fair?!" I shouted, doing a good impression of a killer whale erupting from deep water. "Fair? There are only the three of us *here*. Are you seriously suggesting one of us didn't do this?!"

My subsequent display of rage might have gone on for some hours if not for the sudden emergence of a small seal from the hole in the middle of our sanctuary. It popped its head up and stared inquisitively, if a little blankly, at me. Then returned whence it came.

When it was gone, Sandra said, "Why don't you test the alien baby? Maybe it cut the rope. Why not accuse it, while you're at it."

Dave and Sandra exchanged knowing looks. I'm afraid I turned bright red, from the top of my balding head to my neck. It was clear that they knew my past record. How, I do not know, for it had been stricken as part of the settlement.

I retreated to the far corner of our pathetic square, too impersonal to be called a house or home, and brooded . . . I began to believe, in those moments, that they coveted the alien baby. That there might be some quality to it that I had missed. I picked it up. I spent more than an hour examining it, Dave and Sandra looking on with (feigned, I'm sure) alarm. It bothered me that Dave—and now Sandra—had immediately referred to it as "the alien baby." This naming made me suspicious. Yes, it was green. Yes, it was small in stature. Yes, it did not have a terrestrial physiology—nothing on Earth had features so innocent, legs and arms so stubby. But this did not immediately mean it was an "alien baby." To make such an assertion blended stupidity with an uncanny previous knowledge.

I could not solve the riddle, but I did come to a more heightened awareness of the truth that occurs when people live close together with insufficient chances for attending to hygiene. The mess of cans in the sink. The ever-present fish smell. The funk of human sweat. It occurred to me again that everything I had sought to leave behind had followed me, as surely as if it were a stray dog following a stranger home.

For the next two days, I did not move. I sat where I was and I glowered, thinking. They did not know how to combat this sudden tactic on my part. They joked. They cajoled. They threatened. They appealed to my better nature, my worse nature. Dave said, "Maybe the alien baby is a native Antarctic life form." Sandra said, "Surely, Larry—Dr. Gilchrist—we ought to be continuing with our mission."

Our mission. It had been hanging by a rope, a veritable thread. The thread had snapped. There was no trap, only what had been brought back by the trap. Only our short-wave radio, fizzing and crackling and fizzing some more. It told us of weather and of dim human voices ghosting out of the darkness. And it told us no more.

Then I had the epiphany. On the morning of the third day, I told them to leave. They were startled, astonished even. This final move had caught them unawares. I could smell the stench of indecision on them.

"But, Larry, I mean. I'm not sure you have the authority..."

I waved the rusty edge of an opened can of beans at them. "This is my authority, Dave. This," and lunged at him a little, just to see if he'd draw back, which he did. "And this is my hole," I said, pointing to the hole in the ice. "And you'll do as I say."

Sandra pulled Dave aside then and best as they could they tried, retreating to the farthest opposite corner, a good twenty feet away, to conduct a conversation in whispers. They needn't have bothered. I wasn't listening. I was already back to studying the alien baby. For it had become clear to me that Dave and Sandra were just like the voices on that radio—static-filled distractions. How could I be expected to perform proper research with such dead weight babbling into my ears? How could I possibly begin to understand the secrets of the plastic alien baby so long as they huddled around the cold fire of my research hole?

It seemed so simple at that point, and yet became so complex a moment later. I waved goodbye to them, the alien baby cradled in my arms. They rode off on the snowmobile with nary a wave back, their faces anonymous darknesses behind their snow goggles, their forms reduced to caricatures of Renaissance nudes by the padded weight of their thick jackets and puffy protective layers. They were welcome to those accoutrements of civilization. Me, I would peel off those layers. I would peel and peel and peel until I got to the truth, even a cold truth.

Then it all came undone and went for naught. For, as I watched them metamorphose into a fast-moving dot on the horizon, the alien baby turned its head to look at me and said in a low thin reed of a voice, *Now we begin.*

BULLETS AND AIRPLANES

Introduction

I wasn't always a recluse. I wasn't even confined to this apartment. (There are 3,400 dots on the wallpaper.) No one delivered groceries to me on a weekly basis. And I had a lot of friends. Really, I did.

So how did I come to be in this condition at the tender age of twenty-seven? In a word, statistics.

No messy breakdown. No paralysis of the limbs. No discovery of religion. No birth defects. (There are 200 springs in my bed.)

Statistics. World affairs. Affairs of the heart. The affair of the Woman Sleeping Under the Hill. (The walls of my room are never as close as they seem.)

The Woman Sleeping Under the Hill

She unfolds herself from a fetal position in a cave under the hill and comes to me. There actually is a hill beside my apartment complex: a grassy knoll out of place among concrete, asphalt, neon signs. I am not certain that the woman sleeps under my particular hill, but no one can prove she isn't there.

She comforts me, lets me rest my head on her lap, takes care of me when I'm feeling low. She never says a word beyond "Hush, it's all right." She has no accent. Just curves that fit the curves of my hands, my arms, my body. She strokes my hair and cradles me.

Why do I need comfort?

I could lecture you on the evils of the modern world, but that would be old hat, I'm sure.

The Terrible Weight of Statistics

The Woman told me two stories, through a friend of mine. This friend told me the two stories, but they had her taste to them, her smell.

Two stupid little stories started this whole thing. (People tell me I obsess too much and *that* started this whole thing, but I don't think so.)

The two stories were about life and death.

A Confederate soldier shot a Union soldier through the testicles. The bullet pierced this poor man's balls, shattered the window of a nearby house, and lodged in the ovaries of a Southern belle.

Two months later, the woman discovered she was pregnant. The unlikely couple married and had twelve kids, the other eleven by more conventional methods.

My friend thought this story humorous.

"His testicles," he chortled. "Talk about a shotgun wedding." His purpling face annoyed me; I had a less upbeat opinion.

"The bullet raped them both," I argued. "How you can find that funny is beyond me."

My friend ignored me and told the second story.

It concerned a husband and wife having sex in their second floor bedroom at midnight. In the middle of foreplay, his mouth on her left breast, her hand on his cock, a plane smashed through their window. A Cessna. Twin-engine. I've always felt planes were unsafe.

This I found extremely funny—just the thought of the surprise on their faces, in abstract, made me laugh out loud.

"Oh, shit—there's a plane coming through the window!"

"I'm coming, dear! I'm coming!"

My friend thought I was sick, sick, sick, and declined to tell me any more weird stories. Which was fine by me. I headed down to the library the next day and started looking through books of odd facts. (Did you know it rained turkey innards on Gump, Arkansas, for seven days during the summer of 1859? And that in Starke, South Dakota, over 12,000 bullfrogs overran the local barbershop during the winter of 1970?)

Death. Heart disease, liver cancer, car accidents, plane crashes, train derailings, hurricanes, earthquakes, wars, lightning strikes, shark attacks—it was all there. Check out these wonderful facts from an old National Institute of Drug Abuse survey (annual deaths, mind you): Tobacco, 346,000; Alcohol, 125,000; Alcohol and Drugs, 4,000; Heroin, 4,000; Cocaine, 2,000; Marijuana, 75. Just a few examples so I don't bore you to death. (Bored to Death, 6—all in Kansas.)

It was then that I began to withdraw from the world. Every time I drove, ate something, or took the bus, there was a statistical chance I'd die. Every time a plane passed overhead I'd repeat a litany of *wind shear, terrorists, pilot error.*

Think about it.

Love (and Sex)

I used to masturbate a lot.

Then I met Clara.

Now I masturbate her a lot.

Oh, sure, we make love, too—at least four times a week, all at my place (of course)—but I'm always thinking about the woman under the hill. While we're grunting and groaning and getting all sweaty, I'm thinking about the woman. Can other people see her? How did she get under the hill? Maybe she's some project on cryogenic sleep the CIA did in the 1960s and forgot about. Maybe I should dig up the hill. Maybe digging up the hill would kill her. And what if she wasn't there—what would I do then?

Meanwhile, Clara has climaxed.

"You never say you love me," Clara said on a bright summer day at the zoo, a rare trip out for me, never to be repeated. The baboons were singing to us and the bears were showing us their butts. The zoo keepers appeared to be eating animal feed when they thought no one could see them.

"Well, Clara, I don't," I replied, thinking honesty might please her. "I love the woman who sleeps under the hill."

She threw her popcorn in my face and stomped off in a huff.

Later, we made up. She promised not to get mad when I was being impossible. I promised to see a psychiatrist.

Mortality

I may have lied. I don't believe my current state of immobility can be entirely attributed to statistics. It started much earlier, when I was sixteen. I had read something appropriately existential, nasty, and vomit-inducing (maybe it was Sartre's *Vomit*), and was walking to my grandparents' house when I ran into a post. Not something I do all the time. Really.

It knocked me silly for a moment, but when the moment passed, I was on my feet looking up at the offending phallic symbol, at the top of which flashed a giant AMOCO sign in red-white-blue.

What followed was like the aftermath of a nuclear flash—an instant of true vision.

The sign withered away. The paint crinkled and chaffed off. The metal rusted and corroded. Centuries—a millennium—of erosion took place in about two seconds.

In the end, there was just an ocean of sand from which this pathetic, paintless neon sign proclaiming AMOCO stuck up like the face of Ozymandius, without even the ghost of an explorer to find it. Blistering under a white dwarf of a sun. Beside the sign lay a pile of dust particles which I knew—knew like an ache in my bone marrow, deep in my bloodstream—was *me*.

When I came to, my immediate reaction was to tell the attendant to fuck off after he asked me to stop fainting around his pumps.

"In a thousand years you won't even be dust you glue-sniffing zombie child molester," I said.

"Yeah, you too, you imbecilic motor-function-impaired bull-headed cretin," he shouted back lamely. They don't pick gas attendants for their witty repartee.

But he was right, of course. I had seen it. In far less than a thousand years, I'll be dust. I don't believe in Heaven or Hell. I don't believe in reincarnation. I certainly don't believe in Edgar Cayce, or Mafu, the trans-time personality who spoke in Olde English on Oprah several years ago.

What's left for me?

Friends inform me I'm strange. (They come up to me and say, "By the way, you are one strange puppy.") They tell me that this is the only life any of us have, so we should party all the time, screw as many willing women as possible, and spend a lot of money on our friends.

I doubt any of them have read Kierkegaard. I doubt they've read through tomes of statistics, either.

The Head Shrinker

So I went to see a psychiatrist. His name was A.Y. Tittle and he insisted I call him Dr. Tittle, or "just plain Tittle." Apparently, his first and middle names were invocations of the Devil or hideous jokes bestowed upon him by his parents. Like Asshole Yodeler or Aardvark Yak.

Tittle called the woman sleeping under the hill a "figment of an overwrought imagination."

"Is it at all possible," he asked, scratching his butt with his pen, "that this woman is actually a nurturing figure, like your mother?"

"No," I replied. "I doubt that."

"Why?" he asked.

"Because," I said, staring into his black button eyes, "I've never had a hard-on for my mother."

This response was too direct for A.Y. and the conversation went downhill from there. He was too anal retentive, if you know what I mean.

But he did try, I'll give him that. He even brought up the topic of guilt, which would have proven fruitful if I hadn't kept questioning his denial of carnal lust for his Doberman.

He tried to change the subject, asking me to tell him how I met Clara. I barked at him until he shut up.

A.Y. Tittle was a very messed up guy.

How I Met Clara

I met Clara Mulhoney at a New Year's Eve party. I had drunk too much Scotch, too much rum, too much bourbon. This was before I had really thought everything through and confined myself to the apartment.

One moment I was leering into a friend's face and the next I was in a moving vehicle looking up from the lap of a beautiful woman (Clara) into the face of a beautiful woman (Clara).

As best Clara can reconstruct our meeting at the party, I saw her across a crowded room, noticed she wasn't wearing shoes, and leapt at her toes, pawing and kissing them before puking and falling into a stupor. For some reason Clara thought this was cute.

After that, we figured even if I picked my nose and she talked while she chewed, neither of us could really disgust the other ever again.

Ain't love grand?

An Issues Kind of Guy

Guilt. Oh, I've felt guilty for a long time. Caught like a fly on sticky paper.

I tried to do something about it. I joined the Sierra Club, the Nature Conservancy, Greenpeace. I joined Alcoholics Anonymous even though I wasn't alcoholic, just so I could inspire other members with tales of my heroic sobriety.

But that wasn't enough. Fat fur-clad ladies wearing too much rouge do that much. So I joined PETA: People for the Ethical Treatment of Animals. I walked the picket lines outside animal laboratories. On either side of me three otherwise sane people dressed in giant bunny, puppy, and duckling suits, screamed, "Don't ever vivisect us again! Bunny killers go home!"

Noble sentiments, but when the bunny started telling me about the time it had been beaten with sharpened bamboo sticks, I split.

I tried the anti-nuclear movement, joined protesters who waved banners that read, "YOU CAN'T HUG CHILDREN WITH NUCLEAR ARMS." Across from us stood pro-nuke children. They carried banners that read, "YOU LIGHT UP MY LIFE" and "NUCLEAR FAMILIES DON'T GLOW IN THE DARK." Cryptic answers, I thought. I split.

Next came Greenpeace, but my rubber dinghy deflated minutes before I was to have rammed a Russian whaler.

I wanted to be a radical liberal, dammit, but the best I could do was shoot birds at the president when I saw him on TV.

Now I send relief money to Sierra Leone and the Congo, confident that the rebels there will intercept it and at least someone will use it. Besides, Sally Struthers has such an honest face.

Animal rights, human rights, the environment, they're all the same—doomed to be reduced to a single AMOCO sign in the desert.

My Job

So I got a job. I chopped heads off dead fish for six dollars an hour, ten hours a day, seven days a week. That was fine for awhile—it kept my hands occupied and I didn't have to think about anything but the next *chop* of the enormous cleaver.

Until the fish began to talk to me.

"Tuna," said the first talking fish before I disconnected its nervous system. "Are," said the second despite my feverish chopping, and so on, until they had explained the situation to me: "Tuna are caught using wide-load nets that also kill countless endangered dolphins and sea turtles. We are tuna fish."

I steeled my nerve and continued at the job for a week because I thought paying the rent came before dolphins.

But when the fish started singing in falsetto, I hung up the chopper, threw my blood-stained apron at the boss, and fled the abattoir once and for all.

I was penniless for a week and then Uncle Harry died and left me this apartment and the sum of $320,340.65, after probate.

The money isn't much use. I can't travel—I think I've already mentioned the number of casualties caused by transportation—but I can have groceries shipped in from exotic places. Much safer.

The Family

Uncle Harry choked to death on a rare tuna fish bone. I don't feel guilty. Not one bit. It's coincidence as far as I'm concerned. I was never in charge of deboning.

Uncle Harry typified the family: bigoted, red-faced, long-winded, and rich. Filthy rich, as they say.

He was in the delivery room when I was born. His first words upon seeing me were, "Good God, woman, you've given birth to a lump!" The name stuck.

"Lump," my dad used to say, slapping me on the back, "we're going to the Sudan. Lots of excitement in the Sudan right now, Lump!"

A Hemingway acolyte, my father. A freelance journalist. And off we would go, as if it were preordained that any son of Daddy wouldn't learn about history second-hand, oh no—he would be part of it. Beirut. Pakistan. Brooklyn. We were there. Not always in time to witness violence, but close enough on several occasions.

Mother resembled a gourd in shape and a trombone in timbre, but I loved her about as much as a son can love a gourd. Dad farted constantly, and that was a lot of fun, let me tell you. Especially when you're at the border crossing between Paraguay and Uruguay and the soldiers' fingers are itching at the triggers of their M-16s.

I will say this: they never forced me along any career lines. Perhaps they should have, because I wound up with no career at all. "Be free as a bird," they said. Eagle? Turkey? Maribou Stork?

Good, sound folk despite their flaws, so you can understand my distress when somebody blew their chartered plane out of the sky. They left all the money to dear Uncle Harry.

I was a sixteen-year-old lump at the time, and probably thinking too much even then.

The Woman Again (For Disbelievers)

In my more cynical moments, I realize it is a pretty stupid idea, a woman sleeping under a hill. King Arthur was supposed to be buried and ride out to the rescue, not some anonymous woman. But that was England. No doubt the American version is some deposed beauty queen, some fossil like Zsa Zsa Gabor.

But my lady has emerald eyes and if I look into them long enough, I can see the ocean, can hear the thunder of waves, the hiss of foam on the sand. Her nose is small, her lips full. There's a mole under her left nostril and a fiery red birthmark on her right calf. A certain maturity and wisdom have begun to crease her face.

And music! She sings as if she is an instrument—mournfully, magically. Often, when I wake, I find that tears are running down my face.

And I'm scared. Because when the woman comes out from under the hill, I'm supposed to be cured. I'm supposed to be all better again.

At least a little bit.

A Brief Summation

Inside of this apartment, I have 99 television stations, a VCR, a DVD player, and a CD player, with remotes for all four. I stock caviar, tripe, a variety of non-alcoholic wines. When I am feeling especially Lumpish, I can go down into the bomb shelter with Clara. We make love while pretending we're the last people on Earth.

Clara loves me, but I don't know if that is enough.

In my dreams these days, the sky darkens and the wind picks up over the hill where the woman lies buried. The trees on the hill are dead: their branches thrash in torment. The twigs smack against my window like stray bullets, like sudden airplanes.

When the woman comes to me, she is so old it hurts to watch her approach. Her bones are brittle as the bones of birds, her skin slack, her back bent. Her eyes are stark white, the pupils bleeding away, and when she sings it is like the cawing of crows. As I comfort her—gently take her arm, support her weight—I realize there will be no bullets, no airplanes for me.

Just a slow plodding forward into night.

HENRY DREAMS
OF ANGKOR WAT

"We are not going around looking for opportunities to prove our manhood."

> – Kissinger, 1975, after the last bombing of the Cambodian mainland

Henry has always anticipated the dream that embraces him in his twilight years, these faded years when the diplomacies of Geneva and Paris have become unraveled like an old man's signature. Years of being trotted out on talk shows as an expert, while the bald spot on the North Pole of his head spreads into the tropics.

Before, in the white-hot adrenalin of negotiation, sleepless in the sweat of foreign hotels, Henry had a premonition of the dream: a space at the foot of the bed, occupied by an emaciated Cambodian woman, her side charred by napalm. Staring at him.

"What do you want?" he would ask, groping for his glasses. "Who are you?"

At the sound of his voice, the woman would disintegrate into orange dust motes. Only the eyes remained, a greater darkness in the dark of the night. Staring at him.

"What do you want?" he would ask again.

No answer.

He would realize that he had been awake the entire time.

To the air, to no one: "Dick. It was always Dick's fault. Dick drove me to it."

Always, the bombs fall at the beginning of his dream. They fall like marzipan, like truffles, like chocolate éclairs. Sweets made of steel, humming and whistling as they tumble through the heat-charged air. Images that remind him of the warmth of candy shops in his youth, bakeries and confectioneries. "Please, Momma, a B–52, please, please, please!"

The hum is unfathomable, a sound with such incarnations of power, hidden one within the other, that he shivers, almost cries out against the goose-pimpling of his flesh.

And, more unbearable, more magical, the humming of the bombs is locked inside his head, ready to be released whenever he can gather his nerve.

Henry, dreaming, lost in the Cambodian jungles, dressed in a tux and tails.

At first, the ruins ahead, Angkor Wat, seem a mirage caused by too much humidity, too much heat. Ferns and creepers clutch at him as he approaches along a trail that bleeds moonlight. Prickles of unease stir the hairs on his arms. Crumbling Buddha heads stare at him. The vines crack the solemn features of kings into caricatures of statehood: a nose sliding off here, there a mouth defenseless, disembodied from its host.

Henry climbs among the ruins, his face flushed; he savors his breathing: even and hale, as if he is a much younger man. He hears echoes of *marzipan/truffles/éclairs* . . .

Blocking out the snarl of civet, the scratchy speech of insects, Henry kneels beside a wall that is dark with moss. He carves his name into the porous material: H____ K_____. Just a suggestion of the initials, followed by a straight line, as if his heart had stopped on an EKG. H____ K_____ over and over, until his fingers bleed. There is a bitterness on his tongue that tastes like penance.

Marzipan/truffles/éclairs.

Henry wonders when he will wake up. Henry wonders if he has already awakened.

Beneath a lithe and many-limbed banyan tree, he rediscovers her. Naked, she is thin as before, her left side dark against the brown of her skin.

Henry wants to hide from her, but the wound stops him. It glints in the moonlight like black glass, as if it were a part of her and added to her symmetry. The thought, the possibility, excites him. The sweets keep tumbling through his head.

Unsmiling, she opens her arms to him.

"Who are you?" he asks.

She motions him closer, her breasts pale and touched by beads of sweat. He becomes hard. He awkwardly accepts her embrace. His lips meet hers. The kiss stings. It stings, but the shock arouses him further. She tastes of blood and dust and gunpowder. She tastes of death. *Marzipan/ truffles/ éclairs*; the litany marks his heartbeat, faster, faster still.

She responds to his ever-widening reconnaissance with soft, wet sounds, deepening to an "Ohhh" as he runs his fingers along the wound's outline. It feels crinkly-smooth, like tin foil, or the inside of a sea turtle's cured shell. He leans forward, mouth encompassing one pale breast. His hands move to her thighs. She slides his trousers down. Henry enters her as monkeys howl. They brace themselves against the tree trunk, move rhythmically. *Oh, marzipan, truffles, éclairs. Oh.*

As Henry thrusts, he looks into her eyes, grunts in surprise. Orange. Her eyes are orange dust motes. And old, old as the faces that surround them in the ruins. So old that he wonders again, Who are you?

But (thrusting, deeper) does not ask. The wound on her side bleeds. She writhes beneath him. The eyes dead. Henry whimpers, half-naked in his tails and shirt. His whimpering begs for a reply, but she gives him none.

Henry cries out. Henry shudders. Henry grows limp. Trying to pull himself together, he stumbles away from the woman.

The woman follows him, ghostly now, an orange outline that the wind breaks apart, the specks floating like fireflies in the sky.

He cannot find his signature anywhere in the ruins. He cannot remember his name. He feels the presence of the woman at his back.

"What do you want?"

No answer.

He grows hard again, thinking of bombs falling on Cambodia, the B–52s dark castles that cut the sky, the jungles red with their fury.

When he looks over his shoulder, the woman is gone.

When he wakes up, she stands at the foot of the bed.

Later, on a Sunday talk show, Henry is asked if the U.S. should step up aerial bombardments against Iraq. The hosts cannot understand his reluctance to answer, the quaver in his voice.

The way he stares past them to the monitor, as if he sees something there more hideous than his own image.

A BRIEF SUMMARY
OF SEVEN LOST BOOKS

PAVIC, MILORAD. *Dictionary of the Khazars: A Lexicon Novel; The Hermaphrodite Edition.* New York: Alfred A. Knopf, 2003.

When first published in English (1988), Pavic's *Dictionary* came in Male and Female versions that differed by one paragraph. Revisiting the novel for a special 15-year commemorative version, Pavic has created a "Hermaphrodite" edition that, to accommodate such dual leanings, contains more substantive changes. The following examples are by no means comprehensive.

Page 117: "'If your egg is really all that valuable, why don't you keep it for yourself,' I said, looking him in the eyes . . . " has been replaced by "'Why don't we go for a drink at that bar you like so much,' I said, staring at the pavement."

Page 163: "And so it was from the old man that Masudi received his first instruction in his new vocation and learned all there is to know about dream hunters." has been replaced by "And so it was from the old woman that the cross-dressing Masudi received his first instruction on his new vocation and learned all there is to know about flamenco dancing."

Page 243: "He agreed, and Nikolsky began dictating the dictionary from memory until, at the end of seven days, he had dictated the entire book, all the while eating cabbage with his incisors, which were so long they seemed to grow out of his nose." has been changed to "The idea of racing gerbils had not seemed all that practical to Nikolsky; however, profits had been tremendous and the gerbil track regularly saw more than five hundred spectators a night. Soon they would be rich enough to grow cabbage out of their noses, as the old saying went."

SCHULZ, BRUNO. *The Messiah.* New York: Penguin Group, 2003 (translated by Rebecca Wieniewska).

Long-rumored but only recently discovered in a KGB records vault outside of Minsk, Schulz's novel proves to be a puzzling mix of masterpiece and muddle, dramatically less coherent than alluded to in the author's diary almost 65 years before. The protagonist's midnight ramble through a transformed Warsaw of "de-mechanized" humans forced to hide from intelligent guns, bulwarked by vast bureaucratic guardian demons at the four corners of the city, qualifies as nightmare writ large. The turgid prose conceals images of unbearable sadness and power, as when one of the guardians, dying, metamorphoses into a delicate mayfly of a creature, its song cut short when it is slaughtered by a roving band of "torture animals." When the Messiah of the title turns out only to refer to short-lived day, the reader's very bones groan and shiver. Gone are the themes and the meticulous style set out in such masterworks of the short form as "The Street of Crocodiles." *The Messiah's* closest equivalent emotionally might be William Hope Hodgson's *Nightland*. First published in Poland to intense debate as to the novel's literary merit, subsequent English translations of *The Messiah* have only served to fuel the controversy. Some critics claim the novel is not Schulz's at all, a fact refuted by handwriting analysis.

PROUST, MARCEL. *A Habit of the Knife*. New York: Atheneum, 2002.

Discovered beneath the floorboards of an apartment in Paris where Proust once spent a summer in his youth, *A Habit of the Knife* is nothing more or less than a noir potboiler. Perhaps inspired by a combination of Edgar Allen Poe and Arthur Conan Doyle, the plot concerns the camphor cigarette-smoking detective M. Swann—clearly an early version of the character found in Proust's later *In Search of Lost Time*. M. Swann's journey through the squalid Parisian underground on the trail of a femme fatale who may or may not possess a knife linked to his client's murder is matched only by certain scenes in Verlaine's *Monsieur Phocas*. The prose is remarkable for its hardboiled simplicity and the story moves forward at breakneck speed. The opening lines of *A Habit of the Knife* provide as a good an example as any of the contrasts with Proust's later work: "For a long time, Swann would go to bed so late, the candles would have burned out long before. This particular night, nursing a bullet wound in the shoulder, Swann found his reveries upset by a pounding on his door. Followed by gunfire. It was Combray again. Wanting its money."

GRAY, ALASDAIR. *The Violence Taker.* London & New York: Bloomsbury Publishing, 1972/2003.

An early gang-on-the-run novel, notable for its similarities to Kerouac's *On the Road.* Gray self-published *The Violence Taker* at the age of 17, under the pseudonym Hugh MacThistle ("for the good of all Scotsmen"). Bloomsbury subsequently re-issued the book in 2003. The novel is most notable for the early appearance of the protagonist from *Janine 1982,* beaten up in Chapter 3, "Whereupon A Thrashing Is Delivered, and None Too Soon."

NABOKOV, VLADIMIR. *The Original of Laura.* New York: Alfred A. Knopf, 2002.

Nabokov intended to complete this novel after finishing *Look at the Harlequins!,* but ill health prevented him from doing so. For many years, all Nabokovites had to sustain them were such Laura notes as "Inspiration. Radiant insomnia. The flavour and snows of beloved alpine slopes. A novel without an I, without a he, but with the narrator, a gliding eye, being implied throughout." None of which revealed much about the plot. In 1999, a friend of the Nabokovs—a roving entomologist on a Fulbright—found a series of note cards hidden in the casing of a Nabokov butterfly case donated to Cornell University upon his death. The note cards sketched out a preliminary draft of *The Original of Laura.* Nabokov's son Dmitri then enlisted the help of Martin Amis to complete the novel. In that a first person narrator replaces Nabokov's "gliding eye" and that Amis inserted several seedy characters and changed the setting of the novel to London's underbelly, one might wonder if it would have been better had the note cards remained with the butterflies.

McCARTHY, CORMAC. *Sarah's New Pony*. London: Penguin Juvenile, 1978.

McCarthy's early children's story about a girl's misadventures in the Old West while riding a magic pony mystifies with its blend of extreme violence and adult themes. Trademark McCarthy touches are apparent from the first sentence sentence: "She picked up the stuffed horse. She picked up the stuffed horse. She picked up the stuffed horse as she went out to ride her pony." Later descriptions in which Sarah smashes a bottle over a drunk's head and shoots a revolver wildly into a crowded saloon are sure to puzzle parents, even if delightful to some children. Sequels *Sarah and the Pony in California* and *Sarah and the Pony Ride to Mexico for Tequila* failed as well. Soon thereafter, McCarthy turned his attentions to adult fiction for good.

CARTER, ANGELA. *Eye Candy for Magpies*. New York: Henry Holt, 2002.

Long held back from publication by the trustees of Carter's estate because they feared it might be found lacking next to her other fiction, *Eye Candy for Magpies* may be Carter's greatest novel. It combines the faux realism of such later work as *Wise Children* with the unrepentant surrealism of *The Infernal Desire Machines of Doctor Hoffman*. Set in modern-day London, the novel features Cynthia Gimcrack, a psychologist beset by a series of sudden fantastical visions of such depth and power that she begins to doubt the existence of the real world.

As *Eye Candy for Magpies* progresses, the intensity and duration of the visions increase until her everyday existence, by its very grayness, becomes a terrible pain to her. Inexorably, Cynthia finds herself drawn to this other world, where she can escape the masks she has created for herself in the here-and-now. This transition causes an equal amount of pain in her husband of fifteen years, Mark Gimcrack, but, ultimately, his feelings for her are not enough to bring her back from her destructive path. In the end, it is the overwhelming sense of loss—mixed with the joy for a fantastical world that has none of the fey aspects intrinsic to lesser examples of this type of fiction—that provides the reader with a catharsis almost unparalleled in modern literature. Knowing that Carter had entered the final stages of terminal lung cancer while writing this novel adds an additional layer of sadness to the plot. However, *Eye Candy for Magpies* is bulwarked by Carter's trademark bawdy sense of humor and images so strong that they almost cut the eye in imagined vision.

AT THE CROSSROADS, BURYING THE DOG

The dog lies on your lap, her eyes staring up through the car window at the rain and the way twilight blurs the colors into gray. Perhaps the rain blurs your own eyes, or perhaps you have been crying. In the moistness, flecked with cold, the dog has taken on a thick, sweetish odor. When the car rattles, the backseat rattles too, and your knee shakes, and the dog's head moves up and down so you think maybe the dog did not really die.

But she did die. You heard the whimpering when her back arched unnaturally high. You saw the spasms on the way to the pet emergency service. Later, the phone rang at your apartment and the vet said your dog had died. Listening to the details—palsy, severe dehydration, white blood cell count below five percent—you felt unmoored, cast adrift.

Now the matted fur covers a torso too hollow and legs too limp. Windshield wipers squeaking, the car mutters and jumps and the head moves, the eyes staring up into your face. The colors blur again.

The driver, your boyfriend David, glances back and smiles at you. "She was an old dog, wasn't she?" he says.

David's body tightens with the suggestion of muscles, even

from so slight a movement as leaning back to talk. His taut face wastes neither skin nor flesh; that tightness drew you to him in the beginning.

John sits next to David and nods his head: a tall guy with glasses and a beard. He reminds you of "Shaggy" from the Saturday morning cartoon, "Scooby Doo," and you find him just as memorable. John's an intern at the vet school. You wish he hadn't come along, but he knows David—they played on the same high school soccer team. John has buried many dogs. He knows how it's done, or so David says.

"Very old," you say. Your fingers, thin and cold, run through the dog's fur. You washed and shampooed her three days before her death. With her fur wet, she seemed tiny, her ribs sticking out and her ears flat against her head.

"She was in pain," John says.

"I know she was in pain," you say.

The rain drumming on the car roof cannot soothe the burn in your throat. The dog used to run for hours on the acre you had when you lived at home. She played with an old beat-up soccer ball and grinned through the torn rubber lining. Samoyeds always grin.

David stops in a vacant parking lot. Through the rain, you can see Littlewood Elementary School and the playground where you brought the dog before her legs became so weak she could only stagger. It has been a year since you've seen the playground. Street lamps light the school, but the playground, off to the side, is a series of dark shapes, shot through with glints of metal: slides, swings, teeter-totters.

Hunched over, David gets out. He pulls his jacket collar up to protect against the rain. He opens your door and a sharp, clean smell sweeps into the car, taking away the odor of decay.

David's grip on your arm is firm but gentle. "If we all help, maybe we can get it done faster." For a moment stretched elastic, David, framed by the night and the silver flashes of rain, seems alien to you. Adrift. One of you has been cast adrift.

"Come on," he says. "We'll bring the dog over after we dig the hole."

Something scrapes against the car's trunk. Shovels. John has started pulling out the shovels, clanking them on the car's bumper. He whistles a melancholy, half-familiar tune which catches in your mind and will not let go.

As you close the door behind you, you glance at the dog and think you see the paws flutter, as if she chases squirrels in her sleep, by a fireplace. But the old house on Sixteenth Boulevard never had a fireplace, and certainly not the apartment you moved to when your parents split up. The dog hated the apartment. Cooped up, she shat on the floor. You work fifty hour weeks and the neighbors never helped out. Worst of all, it has no yard, no place to bury the dog.

David suggested you ask the people who bought your parents' house if you could bury her on their property, but what would they think if you showed up, sopping wet, on their doorstep, with a dead dog cradled in your arms?

So you dig a grave in the schoolyard.

Slick with rain, the grass looks black. Nighthawks circle the tall street lamps, snapping up insects. David and John act almost respectful as they dig. It must disappoint David to be here. You were supposed to spend a cheap day at the beach—St. Augustine or maybe Daytona.

"Is this such a good idea?" David asks, breath streaming from his mouth.

"Why not?" You fail to keep the anger from your voice.

"Public property. Security guard's got to be around somewhere."

John snorts through his mouth. "Better a security guard than some psycho."

"Still," David says, and drives his shovel deeper.

If the emergency fees hadn't eaten up your meager savings, you could have cremated the dog for seventy-five dollars, but you don't have seventy-five dollars. You don't even have twenty-five dollars to last the week—and now you're carrying David. He's been unemployed for two months.

The rain becomes wistful, but water still trickles into the corners of your mouth, beads David's forehead. His jeans glisten as if he has gone swimming with them. On a good day, David looks a little like Armand Assante, the actor, but right now he looks tired, irritable, and ugly.

John's shovel strikes something hard and makes a dull, vibrating sound.

"I've hit a root."

"More like bone." David shines the flashlight into the hole. A wide hole, but shallow, with white patches that gleam through the dirt.

"Not bones," says John. "Limestone. It doesn't matter how far from the trees we dig. We're always going to hit limestone."

David shakes his head and smacks his shovel against the limestone patches. You wonder how much of his frustration is real. Maybe he sees this whole episode as something he can tell to his friends in the unemployment office: "Yeah, I spent five hours burying my girl friend's dog. It was dark and cold and rainy and the damn dog smelled like somebody tossed his lunch."

"Maybe the hole's big enough now," you say.

John shrugs and lets his shovel fall onto the grass.

David says, "Maybe it's someone else's turn to carry the dog. Why don't you two go get her?"

You walk back to the car with John, who seems nervous now. He stares into the darkness while he whistles, his hands shoved deep into the pockets of his beige windbreaker.

"How does it feel to put a dog down?" you ask.

The whistle trails off.

After a moment, he says, "It doesn't feel good, but it's necessary."

"People think a lot of things are necessary."

He stops, his back rigid. You can feel his eyes boring down on you and color rises to your cheeks.

"Listen. I'm here as a favor to David. I'm not doing this for the

114

entertainment value."

"It feels good, doesn't it." You cannot look him in the face.

He says, "That dog should have been put down a year ago. It couldn't see. It couldn't hear. It could barely walk. It might as well have been dead. Why did you try to keep that dog alive for so long?"

Silence.

"I thought so."

"Help me with the dog," you say.

You take the dog out of the backseat, her head in your arms, John carrying the hindquarters like he's hauling a sixty-pound sack of potatoes. Somehow, you heft her over to David, who stands by the mound of dirt.

She does not fit the hole. She would not fit the hole even if you bent her in half. The thought makes you nauseous.

David rubs at his left ear, smearing dirt from his hand onto his face. He's beginning to resemble a coal miner. "Come Monday, some little kid is going to get a big surprise. With all this rain, the dog won't stay buried."

He hands his shovel to John and walks over to you. You shine your flashlight in his face, but he hugs you anyway, smelling of sour grass and aftershave. He whispers in your ear: "I'm sorry. I'm really sorry. You know how much I love you." As if that makes it all okay. As if you should just melt into the arms of the fucking knight who has all the answers.

You can't do it. You've never been able to do it. Your spine is too rigid, your jaw too set. All through your parents' long divorce, you set your jaw in anger and defiance. Now your jaw cracks when you chew as a matter of routine.

"I love you, too," you say, but your voice is flat. The words have no relevance to burying the dog.

What does David see in your face to make him frown?

David and John take the dog back to the car, grunting with the effort. Before tonight, you saw her carried only once, when she was eight or nine. She had stabbed herself with a rusty six inch trellis nail. Your Dad was still taller than you and you worried his flanks while he carried the dog into the car. "Be careful! Be careful!" you shouted while he, all action in the form of flesh and bone, drove to the vet.

That was before he left you, when he would romp with the dog and wasn't sullen and moody after work. You could run your fingers through the mystery of his bristly-soft beard and he would laugh deep in his throat and hug or tickle you, calling you, "Little Lizard."

You would brush the dog's fur for hours. You loved the pungent smell of the fur, the coarse-*soft* feel, how it fluffed out at the haunches, longer and sparse at the throat; the rhythmic motion of the brush through that fur.

Back at your apartment, figuring out what to do, you call Dad, with David and John hanging on your shoulder, the dog still dead and stinking in the back seat. You ask Dad if you can bury the dog at his place—a duplex three miles away, with a cat, a backyard, and a new, French wife who replaced Mom.

"Sorry," he says, but doesn't sound sorry at all.

John smokes a filtered cigarette and glances at his watch.

David paces and runs fingers through his hair, finally turns to you and says, "Let's try out by Tower Road. Under a telephone pole or something."

You nod and put down the receiver.

So you trundle yourselves back into the car, with the dog that stinks, fur matted, limbs rubbery. David drives with one hand held over his mouth. You don't bother.

John wrinkles his nose and says, "These things can be traumatic, but it'll be over soon." He gives you a sharp, predatory stare.

You stop on Tower Road at a curve that signals the end of Greenleaf, a residential section with prefab homes and plastic swimming pools, upended and dry for the winter. Half a mile further, the road ends in a waste treatment plant. The rain lingers as mist.

You follow David and John out of the car, huddling around its hood, figuring out a plan.

"First, why don't we move the dog out of the car," David says. "The smell."

You nod yes, tired now: shoulder-sagging, feet-dragging tired. You spent the night and early morning with the dog, worked at your word processing job, and then drove around town collecting David, John, and the dog. You haven't eaten all day. You feel hollow.

David and John bring the dog out of the car. You have wrapped her body in a pink baby's blanket. People might become suspicious. People might think you are burying dead babies all over suburbia. You are not sure whether to laugh or cry.

The dog has gained bulk or David and John have grown weaker. They stagger under the weight. Dad never staggered under the weight.

"Be careful," you say, already too late.

John loses his grip on the head. David flails with the flopping, jouncing hindquarters. The head swings down to hit David in the groin. He swears and drops the dog onto the ground. The head hits first, lolls at an unnatural angle, trapped part-way beneath the body.

John's laughter sounds like the end of the world: a ragged, nicotine-edged rasp.

"I said to be careful!" Anger tightens your stomach; it snuffs out the tears.

David laughs, then cups his groin in mock distress. He gasps, falls to his knees. John leans against his shovel and giggles: Poor Yorick and the gravedigger all rolled up into one.

"What's so funny?" Their laughter makes one corner of your mouth curl upward into an almost-smile. That upward curl pains you; it stinks of betrayal.

David snorts, spins toward John for support, turns back to face you, and says, "Oh, please! The dog is dead! I'm sorry you're sad about it, but it is dead and no matter how we carry her, she'll still be dead."

You hit David. You come at him from the side and punch him in the kidneys and slap his face. "I know she's dead, you shithead! I know that, okay? *That doesn't mean she's gone!*" Your throat feels as if you have been chewing on broken glass.

He grunts in pain and surprise. He falls back, catching you by the wrists. He shakes you—hard. You gasp and make a little sound of pain.

"We're trying to help!"

You both breath like heavyweights between rounds.

"Then why is your stupid friend still laughing?"

"He's laughing at us, not you."

Cars cruise by, some slowing and putting on their brights to see what might or might not be going on. None stop.

Trembling, you untense and straighten up. You should apologize. He tries to help. He means well. All the trite excuses come to mind. Instead, you sit down behind the dog and tug until it lies in a sleeping position. You stroke its fur as David and John dig. You hold the flashlight for them. They dig for twenty minutes. A mound of dirt rises beside them and you are reminded of Richard Dreyfuss' livingroom in CLOSE ENCOUNTERS OF THE THIRD KIND.

David curses; John yelps in curiously dog-like fashion.

"What?" you say, half-rising. "What's wrong?"

"We almost hit a power cable," David says. Or maybe John says it; they stand close together. Resting on their shovels, they resemble wide-eyed owls awaiting some command from you. Above them, the darkness has been stained purple by the quick-moving clouds and the rain, bless it, comes down without warning. You brush dirt and grass from your jeans and say, "Put the dog back in the car. We'll have to find someplace else."

The fatigue has crept into bones, joints, and you groan as you get up. David's hair is plastered to his head in thick, wet plaits. John's watch is so grimy with dirt that he cannot read it, though he squints absurdly at the dial.

David says to John, "Why don't you help me get the dog into the car and then we'll drive you home. It's late." You realize you have embarrassed him in front of his friend.

"Yeah," says John. "It's late."

David drives for twenty minutes through back alleys, angling for the student ghettos behind the university. Silhouettes peer from doorways; hands flash the glow of joints near rows of overturned garbage cans where raccoons have run amok. In the darkness shot through with light your head spins; everything superimposed or a photonegative. Your nerve ends deaden and the dog seems unimportant next to that numbness. You want to open the door and shove the dog out onto the road. You want to hear the thump as it hits asphalt. But you don't do it. You can't do it. Instead, you calm yourself with the rain-song, the dance of water, which your ears transform into the impatient tapping of fingernails on a stainless steel operating table.

Finally, you reach your destination, Sun Bay Apartments. The complex could as well be a run-down Motel 6, complete with rusted gates and overgrown Spanish moss.

"Bye," he says as he lurches out of the car. "It's been real. Sorry about your dog." He nods to you, perhaps wants to say more, but instead turns and jogs up the walkway.

David idles for a few minutes, his window down so the rain comes in, but the smell goes out. The dog's teeth form a snarling grimace and rheum, like pine sap, seeps from the corners of the eyes.

"Do you want to sit in front?" David asks.

"No."

"Where to now?" His fingers tap-tap-tap on the dashboard.

"I don't know." You really don't.

He sighs heavily and stares out the window. "How about a place with sand, like a beach."

"I guess."

"Are you all right? I'm not mad."

"Why don't you drive over to the new soccer fields across town and we'll try there."

"Okay," he says, "the soccer fields."

But your mind isn't on what David says or what you say to David. You remember the times you cried yourself to sleep when Mom and Dad fought, cocooned in the dog's thick fur, her tongue licking your salty hands; the dog's measured breathing, like the slow, steady pulse of the world, letting you drift into sleep no matter how loud the shouts.

At your apartment, you always tried to stay calm around the dog. If you argued with David or were moody, the dog would slink into a corner, its tail down, its mouth closed. The way it looked when Mom yelled at you and said, "I wish you were dead" because Mom really wished *she* was dead.

At the soccer fields, the rain falls without mercy, eroding the packed, sandy soil which will later be seeded with grass—erodes it with torrents and drifts and flurries. The rain beats down on you, the weight of it bowing your back. Your shirt sticks to your bra and your bra feels icy-cold against your breasts. You trudge out with David to dig. You don't know what to say to David; somehow you feel you have nothing left to say, yet you cannot remember having reached a point of no return. Unless it was in the darkness on the way to the John's apartment, driving through the ghettos with John's words repeating themselves over and over in your head: *Why did you try to keep the dog alive for so long?*

"Do you think this will work?" David says. Anything to kill the silence. "It's raining so hard I can't even see with the flashlight. Do you think we should . . . ?"

You ignore him. You dig. Lit by the car's headlights, you dig and try to remember what you are trying to bury. The muscles in your lower back flare with pain and knot together. The grainy wood of the shovel handle gives you blisters and splinters. Your fingernails bleed from the corners of the half-moons. But you continue to dig, until the crash of rain becomes a memory and, finally, the world becomes simple: compressed into the hole you dig, the hole which keeps collapsing in on itself so you feel like

Sisyphus from the Classics course you took before you quit college to get a full-time job. Dad said, Live on your own. Mom is a bad influence. Mom said, Take the dog with you. It was never my dog. It was always your Dad's dog.

You dig and you sweat, despite the chill, and you pant and, most of all, you stare into the hole. After awhile, you see your mother, her dirty blonde hair disheveled, cringing against the livingroom wall at the old house, a kitchen knife in her hand. She sobs like the endless rain of late winter, without passion or the hope of relief, just a slow drone of tears. She holds the knife against her throat. "Come near me and I'll kill myself." Your Dad is a shadow on the other side of the livingroom who says, "Think of the kid for once." He takes a quick stride that eats up half the room. She says, "I *am* thinking of the kid," and increases the pressure on the knife so that her skin tightens and a line of blood creeps down her throat to the neck of her nightgown. "Don't come closer!" she says and you want to go to her, but you can't. You just can't. Instead, you stand there, the dog whining at your feet as though it dreams a bad dream. You hyperventilate and cry at the same time, mucus running from your nose. "Please don't do it, Mom. Please don't." You are invisible to them, your voice sounding small and broken, so broken that it is a wonder you ever spoke again. But Dad comes swiftly close and wrestles the knife away from her before she can use it. He throws it across the room; it slides under the couch. He slaps her. She collapses in a heap against the wall, and screams, "You make me crazy!" Dad walks out the door, slamming it shut. Mom says, "I wouldn't have done it. I wouldn't have done it! Come back!"

You stand in the shadows. You hug the dog with all your strength and you choke on words in your small, broken voice.

* * *

"This isn't working, honey," David says. "This is just not working." His voice sounds worn down to an edge. His shovel drops onto the sand. He shakes you, holding onto you by the shoulders, but you want to dig. He won't let you.

"The hole will keep filling with water. *Will you stop digging!* Look at me!"

He places his wet, grimy hands on the sides of your head, as if he holds something precious he fears will break. His eyes are wide and his body shivers next to yours.

"This isn't working. I'm tired. I've dug three holes. We've driven around for four hours. We have to find a garbage dump for the dog, or leave her here."

You bury your face in his chest. Your hair gets in his mouth as he nuzzles your left ear. "You've done all you could have done. The dog is dead. Let it be."

The rain thrashes both of you, so hard that you fear you will fall apart. His hands are cold on your back. His breathing comes harsh and uneven. He stares into your face as if you have something to tell him.

Adrift. You feel adrift.

You shudder and feel your muscles trying to relax. So it has come down to this, at the crossroads, burying your dog. You remember what John said only hours before: "Why did you try to keep that dog alive for so long?"

Maybe it doesn't matter. Maybe nothing matters except for this moment, when you have the chance to make or unmake your life.

This moment, staring at your boyfriend through the rain, wondering what you are going to say.

AUTHOR'S NOTE

Jeff VanderMeer grew up in the Fiji Islands and traveled extensively abroad. These travels have had a major influence on his fiction. His latest books include *City of Saints & Madmen* and *Veniss Underground*, both of which will be published in the British Commonwealth by Pan MacMillan (Tor UK) in the coming year. VanderMeer's fiction is forthcoming in *The Best New Horror*, among others. Wearing his other hat, that of marine biologist, VanderMeer's studies on the Florida Freshwater Squid have long been considered definitive, garnering praise from the noted squid expert Fred Madnok, among others. He lives in Tallahassee, Florida, with his wife Ann, two cats, and about 4,000 books. Like almost every living soul on the planet, he now has a blog, at:

http://www.vanderworld.blogspot.com

CPSIA information can be obtained
at www.ICGtesting.com
Printed in the USA
LVOW11s0144071217
558809LV00001BA/10/P